HANDBALL!

HOW HENRY'S HAND EXPOSED FIFA'S FAILINGS

Siobhán Gibney & Eugene Gibney

About the authors

Siobhán is an Italian-Irish-Canadian graduate of Queen's University, Kingston, and holds a Masters Degree in Political Science from the London School of Economics. Eugene is a Dubliner, domiciled in Canada, a physician, a lifelong football fanatic, and has a Master of Science Degree in Applied Sport and Exercise Science from Staffordshire University. The authors have published extensively in their fields of professional expertise. This is their first book about football. Eugene is Siobhán's dad.

A Brandon Original Paperback

First published in 2010 by Brandon
an imprint of Mount Eagle Publications
Dingle, Co. Kerry, Ireland, and
Unit 3, Olympia Trading Estate, Coburg Road, London N22 6TZ, England

Published in the United States of America in 2011 by Brandon
c/o Dufour Editions Inc, PO Box 7, Chester Springs PA 19425, U.S.A.

ISBN 9780863224348

2 4 6 8 10 9 7 5 3 1

Cover photos:
Front: Thierry Henry (Inpho)
Thierry Henry (Number 12) keeps his balance after his double handball set up
William Gallas to score the decisive goal (David Winter / Sportsfile)
Back: Giovanni Trapattoni lost in thought near the end of the France–Ireland
match in Paris, 18th November 2009 (Stephen McCarthy / Sportsfile)

Cover design: www.fairwaysdesign.com
Typesetting by Red Barn Publishing, Skeagh, Skibbereen

www.brandonbooks.com

For further information about this book, contact the authors at
18november09@gmail.com

Contents

Authors' Note

We would like to acknowledge all of those who made this book possible, in particular all the journalists, print and photographic, whose extensive coverage of this story has provided a wealth of material from which we have drawn. We would like to particularly thank Sportsfile for permission to use so many of their photographs, and *The Irish Times* for allowing us to use the great "fan reaction" photograph.

We would especially like to thank Benoît Gomis for his help. He assisted greatly with editing and proof-reading, and helped us to access numerous French sources for information. Furthermore, he was our translator, and invaluably gave us the French perspective on many of the issues we examined.

Siobhán and Eugene

July 2010

— 1 —

France qualifies, with an asterisk

ON THE 18TH of November, in the year 2009, in a stadium in Paris, France, a ball bounces off a forearm, is controlled, with a hand, and is passed with one swift kick to a waiting team-mate. The ball is directed into the net, the score is allowed, and it proves to be the deciding goal in a game vital to both teams.

But in what sport, you might ask? What peculiar sport allows you to use your hands and feet to put a ball into a net? Not basketball, surely – no feet allowed. Volleyball requires the ball to be passed over, not into, a net – and even then you are not allowed two consecutive touches with your hand or arm. And the handball association doesn't look too kindly on kicking the ball. But surely it is illegal in association football, the world's most popular sport?

France had qualified for the World Cup finals in South Africa 2010 by overcoming Ireland on a 2–1 aggregate score. That evening, the streets of Paris and other large French cities witnessed scenes of wild celebration by football fans, delighted that their team was going to the finals. But the fans spilling onto the streets of France were not doing so because of this result. They were Algerian fans, delighted that their team had overcome Egypt 1–0 in a play-off to reach the finals. Most French football fans were not celebrating. If anything, they were feeling more embarrassment than joy. The reason was simple. France had triumphed over Ireland in extra time by means of a goal that should have been disallowed. Had the goal been scored despite an unseen offside, or resulted from a questionable penalty kick, many fans might not have paid much attention. This kind of thing happens all the time. The French would have been ecstatic, the Irish left feeling hard done by, but there would have been scarcely a serious mention around the sporting world.

However, the winning goal was scored after a blatant handball (in fact, two consecutive handballs) by France's captain and perhaps best-known player, Thierry Henry. It was apparently not noticed by the referee, either of his assistants, or the fourth official. But it was clearly visible to the nearby Irish defenders, and millions of television viewers in Europe and around the world saw it replayed over and over again from various angles. To add insult to injury, Henry was not shy in celebrating this "goal" in front of the home supporters. For football fans, there was only one conclusion. France had cheated its way to a place in the World Cup finals. Ireland, after what was arguably its best ever international performance in regulation time to overcome a 1–0 deficit from the first leg, was eliminated.

Most sports fans are passionate about the sport they follow – even the term "fan" derives from the word "fanatic". They want their team to win, and at times it seems that they want to win at all costs. But competitive sport has rules, and many fans are indeed experts on these rules. It can be said that many sports have evolved to the stage where most rules are written and codified, but player behaviour and rule-breaking follow unwritten guidelines as to acceptability. A typical football game may have 20 or more fouls, but the fans are well able to make the distinction between a simple foul, and cheating to obtain an advantage. Regardless of team loyalties, people do have a keen sense of fair play, and the French goal clearly offended that sense.

Conscience is a funny thing in sport. Morals, principles: where do they all fit into this multimillion-euro business? The World Cup tournament is held in high esteem largely because players play alongside their fellow countrymen, for national pride, as opposed to playing for club teams, where money is the driving factor. But the role of money in the World Cup, and who qualifies for it in the first place, cannot be dismissed. Millions upon millions of euros were riding on that 18th November game – millions in bonuses, advertisement deals, sponsorships, television contracts, etc. The French team had already booked its accommodation in South Africa before the deciding game. Their 2010 World Cup kit was revealed the following day on the Champs-Élysées. Maybe French manager Raymond Domenech did have reason to be "sure we would be make it through".

Neutral observers tend to support the underdog, particularly if the underdog performs well. Had Ireland played poorly, the football world might not have cared too much how France scored the winning goal. After the play-off draw was made, the Irish team was described by French coach Domenech as the "England B" team – but this "B" team outplayed a French team packed with superstars in the 90 minutes of regulation time in Paris that night. The Robbie Keane goal which levelled the tie was one of which any team would be proud – possession was won in midfield, then came a series of passes with excellent off-the-ball work by the Irish attack, and a cool finish by the Irish striker. And there were other chances too. Even Ireland's (and manager Giovanni Trapattoni's) most vocal critic, television journalist Eamon Dunphy, had only positive things to say about the Irish performance that night. We can imagine viewers across the continent riveted to the game, watching what was supposed to be an easy fixture for the former world champions and current vice-champions (no pun intended), but instead witnessing France in great danger of being dumped from the 2010 World Cup. There is no doubt that most of the neutrals watching were rooting for the Irish by the time extra time arrived. And then came Thierry Henry's arm, hand and pass to William Gallas for the goal – allowed by a referee who was "100% sure" there was no handball, and was 100% wrong!

The play-offs for the European teams resulted in victories for France, Slovenia, Portugal and Greece. Games at this level are typically decided by one or two key moments. Only one team, Russia, scored more than one goal in a game in the play-offs (winning their home game 2–1), and they were eliminated on the away goals rule. Ireland was the only team to score an away goal and fail to qualify.

Even before a ball was kicked in the play-off games, they were a subject of controversy. FIFA made a very late decision to seed the teams in the play-offs. This decision was seen by many as an attempt to make it easier for the teams of France (previous winners of the World Cup in 1998, and runners-up in 2006) and Portugal (containing one of the game's superstars, Cristiano Ronaldo) to qualify. Indeed at the time that the decision to seed the play-off teams was made, Germany was possibly headed for the play-offs too, were it to lose its last qualifier away to Russia. While FIFA may argue that seeding is done to ensure that the top teams participate in the finals, many believe that the real reasons are more financial than sporting, and because of the clout the favoured teams hold in the world of football politics.

Irish goalkeeper Shay Given and assistant coach Liam Brady both went on the record commenting on the decision to seed the teams for the play-off draw. Given described the late decision as "disgusting" and "beyond belief" and in his opinion it was done "because some of the big nations are struggling". Liam Brady pointed out the pressure that the seeding puts on the match referees, saying, "The one thing I hope we get this time is a good referee." There was clearly a perception that regardless of the stated reasons for seeding, FIFA wanted the higher-ranked teams to qualify. "We have to believe that the match officials will be strong and independent-minded enough to ignore any sense that it is France that the powers that be in FIFA would prefer to see in South Africa," Brady was quoted as saying in *The Irish Times* on 13th November 2009. Giovanni Trapattoni later labelled the seeding decision as "treachery".

Although it is the governing body of the most popular sport in the world, FIFA manages to leave itself open to much criticism as to how it runs its flagship event, the World Cup. While the finals take place only every four years, the entire tournament for European teams, from the first qualifiers to the final, does not take more than two years. Yet the rules pertaining to the event are subject to change during this period, at the whim of the FIFA executive. Why are issues regarding seeding not defined at the beginning of each cycle? Making decisions as the event progresses leaves FIFA exposed to the charge of favouritism and unfair manipulation, even if they are innocent of such charges. Following the uproar over the European play-off seeding, FIFA managed to create another controversy by their method of deciding on the seeding for the groups in the finals in South Africa. Despite promoting the value of their world ranking list, updated monthly, it was decided to seed the teams based on their ranking on the October list. The fact that it was long known that the draw for the final groups would take place at the beginning of December was ignored. When France was not among the top seeds, it was suggested that this was in fact a punishment for their manner of qualifying. We do not agree with this view. In the end it did not matter – when the draw was made, France ended up as a *de facto* top seed.

The reader will notice the many issues which have come to the fore following that one night in Paris regarding international football and how it is run. The biggest issue of all, however, is the refusal to allow referees immediate access to video replay in games of importance to ensure fair play. Some even suggest that game results are deliberately kept more open to "influence" as long as video replay is not used. By dragging their feet on this issue, FIFA is already a laughing stock in North America, and risks becoming so in the rest of the world too. As things stand, a World Cup final might well be decided by a missed handball.

The following chapters will explore the most interesting reactions, controversies, and debates that have emerged from that one fateful night in Paris. The facts and issues will be presented in a meaningful and critical way, aiming to make useful suggestions for improving the game. Above all, we hope that football fans around the world will enjoy a good read. The game belongs to us all, because everyone who has ever kicked a ball is a player.

> *Calamities are of two kinds. Misfortune to ourselves and good*
> *fortune to others.*
> Ambrose Bierce

— 2 —

The Boys in Green – wild dreams coming true

WHEN BRAZIL, ITALY, Germany or Argentina qualifies for the World Cup finals, it is considered a normal event, like the changing of the seasons. The details may vary, but the outcome does not. For teams such as England or France there is a certain sense of relief, but of the kind suggesting that entirely appropriate expectations are being met. When Ireland qualifies, it is viewed as an achievement of heroic proportions. It compares to the exploits of the mythical figures of legend. Houghton, McGrath and Keane are spoken of in the same terms as Jason, Ulysses and Fionn Mac Cumhaill.

While the French have had long years of underachievement in the World Cup – described later in this book as a wilderness – the Irish have spent decades lost in a football desert, with hope barely sustained by the occasional mirage of qualification.

The World Cup had been running for sixty years before Ireland's first appearance in the finals in 1990. For many Irish fans it was worth the wait. Yes, those fans! They are the best supporters in the world, without a doubt. In a World Cup qualifier in Paris in October

2004, the huge Irish following participated loudly and enthusiastical-
ly in the singing and humming of the French *Marseillaise*. What
other football fans have done such a thing? Ireland "won" that game
0–0! A French fan suggested to us after the events of 18th November
2009 that if France had been eliminated by similar means, the country would have been alight with burning cars that night. But the Irish
are different. Having waited 800 years for political change, they can
wait a few years for football fulfillment. They believe that their day
will come.

Ireland made their competitive debut (as the Irish Free State) in
1924 at the Olympic Games in Paris, winning 1–0 against Bulgaria.
The Irish declined an invitation to participate in the inaugural World
Cup in Uruguay in 1930. Ireland therefore played its first World Cup
qualifying game in Dublin in 1934, and drew 4–4 against Belgium.
Paddy Moore scored all four goals, and was the first ever player to
score four goals in a World Cup match. A later 5–2 loss to the
Netherlands meant that Ireland failed to qualify for the 1934 finals
in Italy.

Defeat by an aggregate score of 6–5 to Norway meant that
Ireland also failed to appear at the 1938 finals in France. Similar disappointment followed home and away losses to Sweden (for Brazil
1950) and France (for Switzerland 1954). They also missed out on
the 1958 finals in Sweden – conceding a last-minute equalizer to
England in Dublin when a play-off against the "auld enemy" for
qualification looked imminent. Ireland lost all four of their games
against Czechoslovakia and Scotland in the qualifying group for the
finals in Chile in 1962.

The 1966 World Cup finals were to be held in England, where
Ireland would enjoy virtual "home" advantage considering the
millions of Irish who had migrated there over the preceding century

in search of employment. The qualifying group consisted of Ireland, Spain and Syria. After Syria withdrew, Ireland and Spain played over two legs to see who would go to England. (In 1964 Spain had eliminated Ireland in the preliminary round of the European Nations Cup, winning both legs of the tie, and going on to win the European title by defeating the Soviet Union 2–1 in the final in Madrid.) The first game was held in Dublin.

One of the authors admits to being old enough to have attended the first leg game at a Dalymount Park packed with 40,000 fans on 5th May 1965. As recalled, Frank O'Neill launched a free kick towards the Spanish goal from the touchline near the half-way line, not more than a few yards away from where that particular young Irish fan stood pressed up against the wall and fence enclosing the pitch. Under pressure from the inrushing Noel Cantwell, the Spanish goalkeeper allowed the ball to evade his grasp and end up in the net. José Ángel Iribar Cortajarena was credited with an own goal. The image of him kneeling on the goal-line and banging his head off the Dalymount turf in despair is etched in the memory. Ireland won by that single goal.

Spain comfortably won the return leg 4–1, but since goal difference was not used to determine the winner, a play-off was necessary. It was scheduled to take place in London – virtually a home game for Ireland – but the FAI (Football Association of Ireland) agreed to a Spanish request to move the game to Paris. This controversial decision has provoked many a heated debate since, with accusations that the FAI had accepted "inducements" for the switch. So it was that on a November night in Paris in 1965 Ireland was beaten 1–0 by Spain and failed to qualify for the 1966 World Cup. Johnny Giles and Eamon Dunphy played in midfield on the Irish team that night.

Ireland could only manage a single draw in their six qualifying games for Mexico 1970, and failed to make it to the 1974 finals after losing twice to the Soviet Union. Their next campaign was better, but France came out on top of a hard-fought group ahead of Bulgaria and Ireland to book their passage to Argentina in 1978.

By this time, however, Ireland was becoming a force to be reckoned with in international football. This was further illustrated by the qualifying campaign for the 1982 World Cup in Spain. In a tough five-team group with Belgium, France, the Netherlands and Cyprus, from which two would qualify, Ireland only missed out on second place to France on goal difference. Ireland was the victim of poor refereeing decisions in two games in this campaign, scoring legitimate away goals to France and Belgium, both of which were disallowed. The Netherlands, runners-up at the previous World Cup, could only finish fourth.

Ireland disappointed next time out, finishing a distant fourth to an exciting Danish team which went on to impress at the finals in Mexico in 1986. But having come so close in 1982, confidence was growing, and the dream of competing at the World Cup finals was soon to become a reality.

The springboard for qualification came from a slightly fortunate qualification for the European Championship finals in 1988 – with keys roles played by an Englishman and a Scot. Jack Charlton, winner of a World Cup medal with England in 1966, was hired as the Irish manager, and had overseen a good qualifying campaign with only one defeat. Nevertheless it would all have come to nothing if Bulgaria could manage a draw at home in their final game against Scotland, who had little to play for. But Scottish substitute Gary Mackay scored an 87th minute winner for the Scots – and Ireland was suddenly on its way to a place among the top football teams in Europe, and later the world.

If qualification for Euro 1988 left Irish supporters delighted but perhaps a little apprehensive, the Irish performances in Germany were beyond most fans' wildest dreams. Ireland defeated England 1–0, drew 1–1 with the eventual runners-up the Soviet Union, and lost only by a late goal to the tournament winners, the Netherlands. As a result, the Irish approached the qualification group games for the 1990 World Cup in Italy with confidence and high expectations.

Ireland got off to a slow start with away draws against Northern Ireland and Hungary, and a loss to group favourites Spain. Nevertheless, they easily took the second qualifying spot in the group after four successive home victories during which they did not concede a single goal. Ireland, together with thousands of passionate fans, was on its way to the World Cup finals for the first time.

For the second major tournament in a row, the Irish team then exceeded all reasonable expectations. Passage into the knockout phase was secured from a closely fought group after three draws against England, Egypt and the Netherlands. After a scoreless draw with Romania, Ireland then advanced to the World Cup quarter-finals 5–4 on penalties. Hosts Italy proved a bridge too far, winning 1–0, but the Irish team returned home to a rapturous welcome after reaching the last eight in the World Cup in their first appearance at the finals. The fans did not care that the only win in five games was on penalties, nor that the team only scored two goals. The team and manager were all heroes. After decades of disappointment and frustration, Ireland had arrived in football's "Promised Land".

In the FIFA world rankings of August 1993, the Republic of Ireland was listed as the sixth best team in the world. This was two places above Brazil, and ahead of England, France and Spain.

Qualifying for the USA finals in 1994 proved a much more difficult task than getting to Italy had been. Ireland competed in a seven-team group which again included Spain and Northern Ireland, and also a strong Danish team. A 3–1 home loss to Spain in the penulti-mate round of games, while Denmark was beating Northern Ireland 1–0, put qualification in jeopardy. However, in a nail-biting climax to the group on 17th November 1993, Ireland came from behind to draw 1–1 with Northern Ireland in Belfast, as Spain beat Denmark 1–0 in Seville. Spain topped the group by a point, and Ireland and Denmark finished level on points and with the same goal difference. But it was the Irish who qualified because they had scored more goals.

The Irish adventure in the USA began with an extraordinary result in Giants Stadium on 18th June 1994: Ireland 1 – Italy 0. Ray Houghton's 12th minute goal sent the estimated 50,000 Irish fans among the attendance of 74,000 into ecstasy. The three times world champions had been beaten by a spirit, a dream, a figment of wild imagination. Unfortunately, this was to be the highlight of Ireland's participation. The team did make it through to the knock-out round after a loss to Mexico and a draw with Norway, but two defensive errors allowed a much sharper Dutch team to coast to a 2–0 win. Italy recovered to advance all the way to the final, losing on penalties to a relatively uninspiring Brazilian team.

Ireland finished a distant second to Romania in their qualifying group for the 1998 World Cup. An erratic campaign included a shock 3–2 away loss to Macedonia. On this occasion, second place meant that Ireland had to overcome Belgium in a two-leg play-off to secure a place at the finals in France. The Dublin leg finished 1–1, but Belgium won the return match 2–1. Suddenly the holiday plans of thousands of fans for a summer in France evaporated. Nevertheless, this was seen as a transition period, with new coach Mick McCarthy trying to rebuild the team after the retirement of many of the stars of the Jack Charlton era.

The 2002 World Cup was to be hosted jointly by Japan and

Korea. Ireland was faced with a monumental task to qualify, as they were drawn in the same group as Portugal and the Netherlands. The group winners went through, and the second placed team went into a play-off for a spot in the finals. Ireland finished the group undefeated, eliminating the powerful Dutch team by means of a 1–0 win in Dublin. Portugal took top spot on goal difference, but Ireland had little difficulty overcoming Iran after a 2–0 home win in the play-offs, and were off to their third World Cup finals.

Yet again, the Irish performed at a level which seemed to exceed the sum of their constituent parts at the finals. Even more extraordinary was the fact that this was achieved without Ireland's best player and only real superstar, Manchester United's Roy Keane. In what became known as "The Saipan Incident", Keane argued with Irish coach McCarthy and withdrew from the Irish squad days before their first game. The remaining players were able to put this behind them to go through their group undefeated, thanks in no small measure to a dramatic last-gasp equalizer by Robbie Keane against Germany (famously described as being "sucked" into the net by the Irish fans behind the German goal). In the round of sixteen against Spain, Ireland again came from behind to force extra time and penalties, but lost 3–2 in the shoot-out.

Ireland's failure to qualify for the finals in Germany in 2006 was largely as a result of a 1–0 home loss to France (Thierry Henry scoring the only goal), the only decisive game in all the encounters between the four contenders in the group – France, Switzerland, Ireland and Israel.

Ireland lies in 34th position in the table ranking countries by points won at the World Cup finals. Out of thirteen games, they have won two (against Italy in 1994 and Saudi Arabia in 2002), drawn eight (including the penalties win over Romania in 1990, and the loss to Spain in 2002), and lost three (to Italy in 1990, and Mexico and the Netherlands in 1994). In the past twenty years, Ireland has emerged from the obscurity of never having qualified for the greatest show on earth, to making the World Cup finals three times. On each occasion they have made it past the group stage, and given their extraordinary fans plenty to cheer about, and many very precious memories to cherish.

> *Oh the dreaming! The dreaming!*
> *The torturing, heart scalding,*
> *never satisfying dreaming,*
> *dreaming, dreaming.*
> George Bernard Shaw

— 3 —

France and the World Cup –
no strangers to controversy

D ESPITE BEING CROWNED World Cup Champions in 1998,
France have generally had an erratic history in the com-
petition. In contrast to their continental rivals Italy and
Germany, they have in fact frequently failed to qualify for the finals.
This partly explains their great relief in making it through to South
Africa. Over the years, they have produced some outstanding individual players – including Just Fontaine, Michel Platini and
Zinedine Zidane – but as a team, France have frequently underper-
formed. Indeed, it seems to be a prerequisite for the French team to
have a superstar at the top of his game for them to compete successfully at the highest level. The powerhouse teams of Brazil, Germany
and Italy have dominated the World Cup, with Argentina and
England next in ranking. France is ranked seventh in the world in
terms of points won at the World Cup finals.

France participated in the first three World Cups, but the furthest they got was the quarter-final in 1938 – on home soil – when
they went out 3–1 to the eventual winners Italy.

The first World Cup was held in Uruguay in 1930. The host

country held the title of Olympic football champions at that time. National teams were invited to the finals, but only four European countries made the long sea journey to South America: France, Romania, Yugoslavia and Belgium. France played Mexico in the first match, winning 4–1, and Lucien Laurant of France scored the first ever World Cup finals goal nineteen minutes into the game. About one thousand spectators attended the match. However, France lost both of their remaining group games by a score of 1–0 to Argentina and Mexico, and were eliminated. The game against Argentina proved highly controversial. Argentina took the lead after 81 minutes from a free kick. Three minutes later French forward Marcel Langiller was clean through on goal. The Brazilian referee suddenly blew the final whistle, six minutes early. After French protests, the game was restarted but there was no further score.

The next World Cup was held in Benito Mussolini's Italy in 1934. This was the only World Cup where the host nation had to qualify to participate. A total of thirty-two teams made it to the finals, and the competition was run as a simple knock-out event without group stages. France was eliminated in the very first round by Austria. Normal time finished with the score at 1–1, but Austria won 3–2 after extra time.

France hosted the 1938 event in a turbulent world. The knock-out format was used again. France defeated Belgium 3–1 in the first round, but then lost to champions Italy in the quarter-final by the same scoreline.

A world at war had no time for World Cup football, and the next finals were held in Brazil in 1950. This decade saw a gradual increase in France's standing in world football. They failed to qualify for the 1950 tournament, were eliminated at the group stage in Switzerland in 1954, but finished in third place in Sweden in 1958.

France had to play against Yugoslavia to see which of them would qualify for the 1950 finals. Both legs resulted in 1–1 draws, but Yugoslavia won the play-off game in neutral Florence by a score of 3–2 after extra time.

The French beat Ireland twice to qualify for the 1954 finals in neighbouring Switzerland. They did not make it past the group stage, losing 1–0 to Yugoslavia. They did, however, have a consolation victory over Mexico, winning 3–2 through a late penalty.

The 1958 World Cup was very successful for France. The team qualified with ease ahead of Belgium and Iceland with a goals tally of nineteen for and four against. In the finals in Sweden they progressed from the group stage despite a 3–2 loss to their nemesis Yugoslavia, beating Scotland and Paraguay. Just Fontaine scored six of their eleven goals in these three games. In the quarter-final they hammered Northern Ireland 4–0, but lost 5–2 in the semi-final to eventual winners Brazil, with 17-year-old Pelé scoring a hat trick. France defeated West Germany 6–3 in the bronze medal game and Fontaine finished as the tournament's top scorer. Born in French-controlled Morocco in 1933, his thirteen goals at the finals is still a record and may never be beaten. Unfortunately, he was forced to retire prematurely in 1961 due to injury.

Following this success, however, France found itself in the football wilderness for the next twenty-four years. In the five World Cups from 1962 to 1978, France failed to make the finals three times (1962, 1970 and 1974), and was eliminated at the group stage in the two final events for which it did qualify (1966 and 1978). (Table 1)

The resurgence of the French team as a top contender in 1982 could largely be attributed to the influence of one player – Michel Platini. This exciting midfielder later played his club football for a Juventus team managed by Giovanni Trapattoni.

Table 1. France's World Cup Wilderness: 1962–1978

World Cup	Summary of the performance of the French team
1962	Failed to qualify, after a good group phase performance, losing 1–0 to Bulgaria in a play-off in Milan.
1966	Finished ahead of Yugoslavia and Norway to qualify, but eliminated from the finals after losing group games to both England and Uruguay.
1970	Missed out on qualification behind Sweden, mainly due to a shock loss at home to bottom-placed Norway.
1974	Failed to qualify, finishing last in a group of three behind the Soviet Union and Ireland.
1978	Overcame Bulgaria and Ireland in qualification, but did not get through the group stage at the finals after losses to Italy and Argentina.

France qualified for the 1982 World Cup finals by coming second to Belgium in a closely fought group where they edged out Ireland on goal difference, and only two points separated the top four teams. The Netherlands, runners-up in the 1978 World Cup, could only finish fourth.

After struggling through the group stage in Spain in 1982 (they advanced mainly because Czechoslovakia could only draw with Kuwait), France was favoured with a relatively easy second group phase, and came out on top of a three-team group ahead of Austria and Northern Ireland. By comparison, one of the other groups had West Germany, England and Spain, and another was made up of

Italy, Argentina and Brazil! The French were eventually eliminated when they lost to West Germany after extra time and penalties in a controversial semi-final in Seville. They let slip a two-goal lead they had built up in extra time, but the game is remembered almost as much now for the appalling second-half foul committed by German goalkeeper "Toni" Schumacher on French player Patrick Battiston. The French player was stretchered off with serious injuries, and the referee awarded a goal kick in what *BBC Sport* still lists among the "world's worst refereeing decisions". Michel Platini was later reported to have said that he had thought Battiston was dead after the collision. Schumacher's foul went unpunished, and he stayed on the pitch to save two penalties in the shoot-out to help West Germany reach the final.

France won the European Championships held in France in 1984, and this golden era continued when a Platini-inspired France finished third in the 1986 World Cup in Mexico. France qualified for the 1986 finals by heading a closely fought group with fellow-qualifiers Bulgaria, ahead of East Germany and Yugoslavia. The French started the event as one of the favourites to win the World Cup, but it was not to be. After easing through the group phase with victories over Canada and Hungary, their excellent performances included knock-out round victories over Italy (2–0) and Brazil (on penalties), before losing to West Germany again in the semi-final. Argentina, inspired by Diego Maradona (whose handball goal against England in the quarter-final has never been forgotten), won the final 3–2.

The following years were lean ones again for France, when it failed to qualify for either the 1990 World Cup finals in Italy, or the USA event in 1994. In the attempt to qualify for the 1990 event, an early dropped point away to Cyprus proved decisive as France lost out on the second qualifying place to Scotland by one point, in a group dominated by Yugoslavia. Failure to qualify for the USA was particularly hard to swallow for French fans. Indeed, it was an event at least as traumatic for them as Ireland's exit from the 2010 World Cup was for Irish fans. The French had all but secured qualification, needing a single draw from their last two games, both at home. With a team of stars including Eric Cantona, David Ginola and Jean-Marie Papin, they seemed to have everything under control when a superb Ginola goal gave them a 2–1 half-time lead against Israel, the last-placed team in the group. But they lost 2–3, conceding the winning goal in the third minute of injury time. Worse was to follow when they lost also to Bulgaria (1–2), with Emil Kostadinov scoring the winning goal in the last minute of play to eliminate the French. David Ginola was vilified for conceding possession to the Bulgarians from an overhit free kick which led to their counter-attack and winning strike.

As host nation, France was not required to qualify for the 1998 finals. Zinedine Zidane inspired France to finally win the World Cup in Paris in 1998, and the squad, which included Thierry Henry, certainly impressed throughout the event.

France won all three of their group games, scoring nine goals and conceding only one. Twenty-year-old Henry scored three of these goals. In the match against Saudi Arabia, which France won 4–0, Zidane received a red card and a two-game suspension after stamping on an opponent. This violent side of Zidane's character was to re-emerge on the world stage eight years later in the World Cup final against Italy.

In the knock-out phase, things were a bit more difficult. France beat Paraguay 1–0 with a golden goal in extra time, and then overcame Italy in the quarter-finals on penalties after a scoreless draw. Two goals from defender Lilian Thuram gave them a comeback victory over Croatia in the semi-final.

Their World Cup final victory over Brazil was not achieved without a background of controversy – but one exclusively Brazilian in origin. Their star player Ronaldo had suffered a mysterious convulsive illness prior to the game. He was omitted from the original team sheet, but then re-instated. He had a very poor game, and the morale of the whole Brazilian team was adversely affected. This had as much to do with determining the outcome of the match as Zidane's two-goal performance in a comprehensive and well-deserved 3–0 victory for the hosts. Thierry Henry did not play in the final.

France continued their winning ways to become European Champions for the second time in 2000, beating Italy in the final. Previously only West Germany, by winning the World Cup in 1974 after their European Championship triumph in 1972, had held both of these titles at the same time. Most recently, Spain joined this exclusive group by winning the South Africa World Cup. As World Cup holders the French were not required to qualify for the next World Cup, and they headed to Japan in 2002 full of confidence. However, they were soon on the plane home, after defeats to both Senegal and Denmark and a draw with Uruguay. They failed to score a single goal in the event, sharing this distinction with China and Saudi Arabia.

French attempts to qualify for the 2006 World Cup finals in Germany got off to a shaky start. They failed to win any of their home games against rivals Israel, Ireland and Switzerland. Only after the return from retirement of Zinedine Zidane, Claude Makélélé and Lilian Thuram did the campaign take off. A key 1–0 victory in Dublin proved to be the only game involving the four contenders for qualification that did not end in a draw. France and Switzerland made it to the finals. In Germany, France staggered into the knock-out rounds after group phase draws with Switzerland and South Korea, and a win over Togo. Then, inspired by a resurgent Zidane, the French surprised everyone (including themselves) by a sequence of wins over Spain, Brazil and Portugal to reach that eventful final in Berlin against Italy. The result hinged mainly on the contributions of two players. Zidane scored for France from the penalty spot in the first half after Marco Materazzi was adjudged to have fouled Florent Malouda. Zidane was then red-carded in extra time after head-butting Materazzi. On the other hand, Materazzi scored Italy's equalizer in the game, and went on to score one of the goals in the penalty shoot-out won by Italy. In an interview published in *France Football* late in 2009, Zidane indicated that he was glad to have been sent off because otherwise he does not know how he could have "lived with it had France become world champions and I had stayed on the pitch" after what happened.

So, while they have tasted victories in two European Championships and a World Cup, French fans and players have had to endure some especially traumatic defeats – notably against West Germany in Seville in 1982, and in their failure to qualify for USA 1994. After the controversial qualification for South Africa, however, the French players had to cope with a particularly painful victory. How they managed became a whole new and sorry chapter for French football.

> *You have to learn the rules of the game. And then you have to play better than anyone else.*
> Albert Einstein

— 4 —

French connections – the historical perspective

I RELAND AND FRANCE played against each other thirteen times before they were drawn to face each other in last chance qualification play-offs for the 2010 World Cup finals. They played six times in Paris with France winning three times, two games being drawn, and the Irish winning their very first encounter, a friendly in 1937. Of the seven games in Dublin, Ireland has won three, two were drawn and France won twice. So, against a nation which has won two European Championships and one World Cup, the overall record is not a bad one for the Irish (P:13, W:4, D:4, L:5, F:14, A:16). Of these thirteen games, three were friendly matches, but the remaining ten were World Cup qualifiers. Ireland and France have never played each other in the European Championships or at the World Cup finals.

The 1954 World Cup finals were to be held in Switzerland, and Ireland and France found themselves in a three-team group along with minnows Luxembourg. The group winners would advance straight to the finals. In the first match at Dalymount Park in front of 45,000 spectators, the French were clearly a more skilful team and raced to a

5–1 lead, with two late goals for the Irish making the score a bit more respectable. One of the French stars was Raymond Kopa, later to play a key role in France's third place finish at the 1958 World Cup finals, where he was named Best Player of the Tournament. France won the Paris game 1–0 and with both teams defeating Luxembourg twice, it was France that finished a clear first in the group.

The sides were not to meet again for almost twenty years, when again they had to compete for a place at the World Cup finals, this time to be held in Germany in 1974. Ireland won the first of their two games, in Dublin, by a score of 2–1. This was Ireland's first home victory against anybody in six years. The Paris match ended 1–1 after a pair of late goals. Raymond Domenech played on the French side that day. However, the three-team group was dominated by the Soviet Union, who defeated Ireland twice and France once to head the group. But the Soviets never did make it to the finals. They needed to defeat Chile in a two-leg play-off, but after a scoreless draw in Moscow, they refused to travel to Chile for the return leg in November 1973. The reason? General Augusto Pinochet, backed by the USA, had staged a *coup d'état* in September against the elected government of Salvador Allende.

Ireland and France were now becoming regular opponents in their attempts to qualify for the World Cup finals. They were drawn together again in the very next cycle. This time Bulgaria was the third team in the group vying for a place at the 1978 finals in Argentina. France won their home leg 2–0 against Ireland with Michel Platini scoring one of the goals, but Ireland managed a 1–0 win in Dublin. Liam Brady scored the goal. The group winner was decided by the results against Bulgaria. France won at home and drew away, while Ireland only drew at home and lost away. In the end, France was first, and Ireland last.

Inspired by Platini, the French team was by this time developing into a real force in world football. For the third time in a row, France and Ireland were drawn in the same qualifying group. The finals were to be held in Spain in 1982. This time it was a five-team group, with two teams qualifying. France won the Paris game by two goals to nil. Trailing 1–0, Ireland was denied a legitimate equalizer when a Michael Robinson goal was disallowed. Kevin Moran had been wrongly adjudged to have handled the ball in the build-up to the goal. A subsequent 3–2 victory for Ireland in Dublin must rank as one of Ireland's best ever international wins, although even after this loss, France was still in the driving seat with two home games remaining to finish their campaign. This was the French team that was soon to lose a World Cup semi-final so cruelly to West Germany in Seville in 1982. In fact, this was an exceptionally strong group, and Ireland's campaign also included a home win and an away draw against the Netherlands. Ireland failed to qualify only on goal difference. France had racked up an 11–0 goal tally over two games against Cyprus, but Ireland had only managed 9–2. The final table (Table 2) shows that the Dutch, beaten finalists in the previous two World Cups, could only finish fourth. Strangely, the group winners Belgium had the worst goal difference of the top four teams.

Table 2. World Cup 1982 Qualifying Group 2

	P	W	D	L	F-A	Pts
Belgium	8	5	1	2	12–9	11
France	8	5	0	3	20–8	10
Republic of Ireland	8	4	2	2	17–11	10
Netherlands	8	4	1	3	11–7	9
Cyprus	8	0	0	8	4–29	0

After this, the two teams took a break from each other, during which France of course went on to win the World Cup in 1998. It was not until the qualification campaign for the 2006 World Cup in Germany that Ireland and France were again drawn together in the same qualifying group. This very competitive group also included Switzerland, Israel, Cyprus and the Faroe Islands. The Paris game was played first and was noteworthy for two reasons. Firstly, the Irish performed very well in a 0–0 draw, and might even have won the match, with the most clear-cut chance of the game falling to John O'Shea in the second half. The second remarkable feature of the game was the level of Irish support in attendance. It is estimated that between 25,000 and 30,000 Irish fans were among the 79,000 spectators at the Stade de France that night.

The Dublin match in 2005 was a different story. With Zidane, Makélélé and Thuram back in the team, France managed a 1–0 victory through a second-half strike from Thierry Henry. This result proved to be the only decisive game between the top four teams in the group. France and Switzerland progressed, with the French going on to a second place finish at the finals. Ireland was back in the familiar situation of pondering what might have been.

Over the years, the games between the two teams have been characterised by competitiveness and sportsmanship. Most of the decisive games have been decided by a one-goal margin. No player has ever received a red card during an Ireland-France game. There have been only three bookings in the entire series of games between these two sides, excluding the game in Dublin in 2005 when six yellow cards were shown. Other football rivalries are not so benign, with the series of England-Argentina games down through the years serving as a good example. Perhaps this comparison is not entirely fair, as Ireland and France have never been at war with each other, and the two countries have more often than not been sympathetically aligned by their mutual feelings towards the English.

Of the other major international sports, Rugby Union is the one which has the most extensive history of rivalry between the two nations. Of the 86 encounters, France has won 52, with only 29 wins for Ireland and five draws. The teams have met three times at the Rugby World Cup finals, and France has won each time. In the quarter-finals of 1995 the score was 36–12, and in 2003 they won by 43–21. In 2007 France defeated Ireland by 23–3 in a group stage game at the finals. Incidentally, in recent years, rugby and football internationals between the two sides have been held at the same venues.

Naturally, the connections between Ireland and France are not confined to sport. Historically, there are clear links between the French and the Irish. As far as conflict is concerned, however, they tend to be united, particularly when the enemy is English.

Large-scale Irish emigration to continental Europe was common from the mid-1600s onwards. The Irish left home for a number of reasons: following military defeat, to avoid religious persecution, and for economic reasons. While initially Spain was the destination of choice, later France provided a natural haven. Irish colleges and seminaries sprung up in France, and Irish soldiers ("Wild Geese") eventually collected to form France's Irish Brigade. Estimates suggest that over 500,000 Irishmen died fighting for France in the hundred years prior to the dissolution of the Brigade in 1792.

The military exploits of these times were the stuff of heroic tales and poetry. The French victory at Fontenoy over the "Pragmatic Army" in 1745 was achieved with a significant contribution by the Irish.

The French Revolution was certainly an inspiration to many Irishmen seeking to break ties with England. In the late 1700s Wolfe Tone persuaded the French to ally with Ireland and send men and arms to support an Irish uprising against the English. On 15th December 1796, a French fleet commanded by Houche set sail from Brest with 15,000 men. A combination of poor seamanship and bad weather prevented it from landing in Bantry Bay, and by mid-January the fleet had returned to France. Another attempt later in 1797 to provide French aid to the Irish cause met with a naval defeat of the Dutch fleet (which supported France) by the English at Kamperduin.

French assistance to the Irish rebellion eventually arrived in August 1798, by which time the rising had already been almost crushed. It was too little and too late. A French force of roughly one thousand men under General Humbert did land in County Mayo. They were joined by local rebels, and had some initial success, but were defeated at the Battle of Ballinamuck on 8th September. The following month, a larger French force accompanied by Wolfe Tone himself attempted to land in Donegal. They were defeated by a superior British force and Tone was captured. The United Irishmen Rebellion was over. Napoleon Bonaparte did not pursue the idea of military aid to Ireland when he assumed power in France. Since then, Irish and French history have gone along quite separate paths.

Evidently, there is no historical or sporting "bad blood" between these two close neighbours on the western shores of Europe. (At least there was not any until 18th November 2009!) They are simply two countries divided by a body of water and a barrier of language, but united by a certain antipathy towards the English and a strong sense of sportsmanship and fair play. Ireland might indeed be regarded as one of the lesser footballing nations that the French traditionally have had a great deal of trouble beating. And still do.

> *No matter where; wise fear, you know,*
> *Forbids the robbing of a foe;*
> *But what, to serve our private ends,*
> *Forbids the cheating of our friends?*
> Charles Churchill

— 5 —

All roads lead to Paris

IT IS NOT all that easy to qualify for the World Cup finals. Nowadays, the only team guaranteed a place is the host country. Only for the 1934 tournament in Italy were the hosts not automatically given a spot. Ever since the 2002 finals, even the defending champions are obliged to qualify. Looking at the October 2009 FIFA rankings, we notice that three of the teams in the top twenty places, Croatia, Russia and the Czech Republic, have all failed to qualify for South Africa 2010. Brazil is the only team to have played at every World Cup finals. Argentina has qualified for every World Cup finals when they participated, but they did not take part in the competition in 1938, 1950 or 1954. Similarly Germany (including the former West Germany) did not partake in the 1930 and 1950 events, but otherwise has always qualified. Italy has always made it to the finals but did not partake in the first event in 1930. However, not all former World Cup champions have been so consistent. England, the winners in 1966, did not qualify in 1974, 1978 or 1994. France and Uruguay, both former champions, have each failed to qualify six times since 1950.

Only 55 countries (out of 203) have qualified for more than one World Cup final tournament.

Both Ireland and France thus approached their qualifying groups for South Africa 2010 somewhat cautiously and apprehensively. Ireland had failed to make it to the World Cup finals in Germany in 2006, and had a disastrous campaign in their attempt to qualify for the European championships in 2008. They finished a full 10 points behind second placed Germany (Czech Republic topped the group), and suffered a humiliating 5–2 loss away to Cyprus. Prior to this, Cyprus had never even managed a draw against Ireland. In addition, Ireland only managed to beat lowly San Marino by means of a 94th minute goal, and also required an injury time goal to prevent them from losing to Cyprus for the second time. Giovanni Trapattoni inherited a squad low in confidence when he took over at the beginning of the World Cup qualifying campaign.

In the qualifiers for the 2010 World Cup, Ireland was drawn in Group 8 headed by world champions Italy, along with Bulgaria, Cyprus, Montenegro and Georgia. Realistically, the most the Irish could expect was a second place finish and a place in the play-offs. In the end they managed this fairly comfortably if uninspiringly, through a combination of good fortune, some gritty displays, and a poor campaign by Bulgaria.

Ireland's two wins against Georgia were achieved with considerable help from outside influences. Georgia's home tie against Ireland was moved to Mainz, Germany, after the outbreak of war between Georgia and Russia. This loss of home advantage was fully exploited by Ireland, who won 2–1. Later, in the Dublin game, the Georgians were leading 1–0 when Ireland was mysteriously awarded a penalty, which turned the game around. Ireland again won 2–1. Two single goal victories against Cyprus were enough to see the Irish into second place, after drawing home and away against both Bulgaria and Italy. Bulgaria had their own Cypriot tragedy, losing 4–1 in Larnaca, although they were already all but eliminated at that stage. Ireland was the second placed team with the eighth best record among the runners-up in nine European groups (Table 3). Norway was eliminated.

So Trapattoni's team had made it to the play-offs undefeated. It is of course difficult to go through the process of rebuilding a team and also to achieve the necessary competitive results at the same time. And for many Irish fans, they were not sure if the team was really getting good, or had just stopped being bad.

France started their World Cup qualifying campaign also low on confidence. They had performed poorly at the European Championships in 2008, gaining only one point from a scoreless draw with Romania, losing 4–1 to the Netherlands, and 2–0 to Italy.

France was still the top-seeded team in its World Cup qualifying group, and seemed to have it well within its reach to finish first and get a ticket straight to the finals. The other teams in France's qualifying group were Serbia, Austria, Romania, Lithuania and the Faroe

Table 3. World Cup 2010 – European Qualifying Groups

Second-placed teams	Points won against other top five teams in group (8 games)
Russia	16
Greece	16
Ukraine	15
France	15
Slovenia	14
Bosnia and Herzegovina	13
Portugal	12
Republic of Ireland	12
Norway (did not qualify)	10

Islands. France got off to a shocking start with a 3–1 loss to a mediocre Austrian team in Vienna, on the same night that the once powerful Romanians were showing how far they had regressed, losing 3–0 at home to Lithuania. The French made some amends only four days later, beating Serbia 2–1 at home, and the loss to Austria was to be their only loss in the group. But they failed to impress as the group took shape, squeaking past Lithuania (twice) and the Faroe Islands, each time by a single goal, and drawing twice with Romania. Despite two convincing home wins to conclude the campaign (if a home win over the Faroe Islands can ever be considered convincing), they could only finish second to Serbia. For this stuttering performance in the group in which they were the top-seeded team, France was rewarded by the FIFA decision to seed the teams again for the play-off games between eight European runners-up.

Both teams therefore approached the play-off games with a sense of fear and trepidation. Ireland knew that it would inevitably have to overcome a difficult opponent to reach the finals. The French had concerns about their own poor form.

Giovanni Trapattoni did not make any statements when the seeding decision was announced, but would later call this "treachery". Meanwhile, Shay Given called it "disgusting", and Liam Brady was concerned about the possible effects of the seeding on the play-off referees. It was obvious that the officials would be aware of which teams FIFA preferred to have at the World Cup finals. Clearly, the Irish camp did not relish the prospect of having to play against one of the stronger teams remaining. When it proved to be France, the highest-ranked team of the eight, it seemed that Ireland's worst fears had come true. To make matters worse, the second leg was to be played in Paris. Many Irish supporters believed that the team was all but eliminated before a ball was kicked. The only glimmer of hope was that Ireland was proving ever more difficult to beat. After all, even world champions Italy had failed to do so in two games. If Ireland could avoid giving up a goal in Dublin, there was still hope.

The French were none too happy about the pairing either. While most commentators thought that the team should have little difficulty getting past Ireland, there was still a certain amount of apprehension. Many felt it might not be so easy to overcome the Irish. Despite a marked disparity in the respective football achievements of the two countries and a gap of twenty-five places between the teams in the FIFA rankings, Ireland had always been a difficult opponent for France. Of their previous thirteen encounters, France had won five, Ireland four, and the other four were drawn. The French also recognised the important role played by the passionate Irish supporters, and remembered the huge Irish following that had attended the World Cup qualifier in Paris in 2004. A home federation is required to supply 10% of match tickets to the visitors, and this time the French were determined that Irish support at the Stade de France would not be much higher than the 8,000 in accordance with this obligation. In fact, after initially announcing that the match tickets would be sold online, the tickets eventually went on sale at various outlets in France instead. At times it seemed that the French were a little too respectful of their opposition, almost to the point of making their own task psychologically harder. After all, the French team was full of top-class players, playing in Europe's best club teams and competing regularly in the Champions League. Ireland's team could not boast such a line-up. But Ireland was still not England B! It was said that Ireland was stronger than France in only two positions: goalkeeper and manager.

The first leg of the tie was played in Dublin on Saturday 14th November 2009. Ireland clearly had the better of the first half, and

France created few goal-scoring chances. Ireland's best chance fell to Liam Lawrence, but Patrice Evra got the slightest touch to deflect his close-range effort just wide. Both sides had chances in the second half, but the game was decided by a single goal, scored by French forward Nicolas Anelka, whose shot deflected into the net off Seán St Ledger in the 72nd minute. The French goalkeeper Hugo Lloris made a key save when he came out to deny Glenn Whelan with just four minutes remaining.

At the end of the game, Ireland's Keith Andrews was involved in an "argument" with France's Lassana Diarra. Words were spoken, and some shoving and pushing ensued. "Handbags at twenty paces," as these things go. Apparently Diarra had made some derogatory comments about Ireland's chances of winning the fixture after France's victory. But the Irish needed no additional motivation for the return leg in Paris. They were playing for World Cup survival. For some players it would be their last chance, and for others, possibly their only chance.

Despite the defeat, manager Trapattoni remained upbeat about Ireland's chances. He felt that the Irish performance had been a good one, and that the team was well capable of scoring in Paris against a French team that did concede goals, home and away. The day after the match in Dublin he said: "We have to think about the positive situation and not the result because in the end, football can come down to a deflection, the crossbar, the referee — there are many situations which can change the result."

Teams which require only a draw in a home game often have difficulty in their approach to such a game. Brazil and Uruguay met in the decisive final match of the 1950 World Cup. The winners of a group phase of four teams would become world champions. Brazil had comfortably defeated Sweden (7–1) and Spain (6–1), whereas

Uruguay had only managed a 2–2 draw with Spain, and had beaten Sweden by a single goal, 3–2. However, in front of an estimated 200,000 spectators at the Maracanã Stadium in Rio de Janeiro, Uruguay came from behind to defeat Brazil by a score of 2–1. More recently, the French themselves had faltered at home in their attempts to qualify for the 1994 World Cup finals. Needing a single point from their remaining two games to qualify, they managed to lose twice at home, to Israel and to Romania, conceding late goals in both games. French goalkeeper Bernard Lama reflected later: "We didn't know whether to go for a win or a draw. We were caught between two stools."

For most neutrals, however, the France–Ireland play-off tie was as good as over. But the Irish had fashioned exceptional performances in difficult circumstances in the past and were not out of it yet. In fact, it was probably to their advantage in one way that they were going to Paris 1–0 down, rather than at 0–0. Ireland had nothing to lose, and if they managed to score first, it was game on. On the other hand, how would the French approach the second leg? Should they play with caution and hope for a scoreless draw? Or should they be more aggressive and try to kill off the tie, at the risk of leaving themselves exposed to a counter-attacking strike by the Irish? The scene was set for what was to be one of the most controversial games in the history of World Cup qualifying matches.

Without measureless and perpetual uncertainty the drama of human life would be destroyed.
Winston Churchill

— 6 —

Paris Match – report and analysis

THE SECOND LEG of the play-off tie between France and Ireland took place at the Stade de France, Paris, on 18th November 2009, and kicked off at 9pm local time. Neutral observers gave Ireland little chance of overturning the goal deficit from the home leg. France was the hot favourite, if not to actually win the Paris match, at least to do enough to emerge the overall victors and qualify for the World Cup finals. The stadium was full to capacity, including an estimated 10,000 to 12,000 Irish supporters. The French tried to encourage support from the home fans as much as possible by placing a French flag under every seat. The announcer led the chanting before the kick-off: "I'm going to shout 'Allez les bleus' and then you follow." The game about to begin was to prove to be one of the most talked-about World Cup qualifiers ever.

There were no changes for Ireland from the team that had lost in Dublin four days earlier. France made one change in their line-up. Eric Abidal was injured, and was replaced by Julien Escudé.

The early minutes passed without major incident, with Ireland at least getting the ball into the French penalty area a couple of times, but without any real threat. After seven minutes, French defenders Evra and Escudé then collided going for the same ball, and Evra's elbow made contact with Escudé's face. Sébastien Squillaci had to replace the bleeding Escudé. Each side then mounted several tentative attacks, trading a few corners that came to nothing. After 20 minutes, there were no real goal-scoring chances, and the exchanges had been roughly equal. Neither team had dominated, but Ireland was winning enough midfield possession to be encouraged. They had certainly not been outplayed so far.

The first scary moment for the French arrived after 24 minutes. Liam Lawrence and Kevin Doyle were both involved in the attack. Robbie Keane followed up, but French goalkeeper Hugo Lloris timed his move off the line to perfection to scoop the ball off Keane's foot just as he was about to make contact. The Irish gained in confidence from creating this real chance, as did Lloris for dealing with it so well. Within two minutes Ireland created another great opportunity. Lawrence floated in a precise cross from the right, and Doyle got to it ahead of William Gallas. However, Doyle made a poor contact with the ball, and his header went harmlessly wide.

Ireland then went deservedly in front after 33 minutes with a goal of simplicity and precision. John O'Shea won possession for Ireland in midfield, and Kevin Kilbane and Damien Duff exchanged passes down the left flank. A pinpoint angled ball from Kilbane found Duff taking control near the goal line at the edge of the penalty area. Keane, waiting in the middle, quietly dropped back off his marker, and Duff found him accurately enough for Keane to side-foot the ball to his right and into the corner of the net. Lloris had no chance. The Irish had scored the away goal they needed, had played well so far, and suddenly had every reason to believe that a place in South Africa was again within their grasp. We all recall the near-silence that sometimes greets a goal by an away team. The Irish fans did not let this happen here, and the stadium was filled with their deafening support. Robbie Keane celebrated his clinical strike with a quizzical look on his face that seemed to say, "All too easy, don't you agree?" The goal was certainly made easier by lax French defending, which failed to mark first Duff and then Keane, in the attack.

The remainder of the first half played out without any major threat to either goal. The French edged forward a few times after conceding the goal, and after 40 minutes André-Pierre Gignac failed to get control of the ball when in a decent shooting position. But the French did not demonstrate any incisiveness in attack, and Ireland still gave as good as they got in this period. A long-range Glenn Whelan free kick in added time cannoned off Evra and away for a corner.

The French went off at half-time to the sound of derisory whistles and boos from their own supporters. They had failed to create a single clear-cut chance in the entire half, and it reflected fairly accurately on their performance that their best player was goalkeeper Lloris. The Irish had played exceptionally well, scored the only goal, and had created a couple of other half-chances. They were hungrier to gain possession, and won most of the 50/50 balls. They were the dominant team in midfield, and gave away little at the back. Although they still relied to some degree on a long-ball game, it proved effective. The French central defence looked decidedly shaky, and repeated pressure often is rewarded in such circumstances. Indeed the Irish goal came at the end of a ten-minute spell in which they had created two goal-scoring chances.

However, there were still 45 minutes, or more, to play, and a lot at stake. Would Ireland be able to maintain their high level of performance in the second half? Would France finally come good and live up to their favourite tag? After all, they had a world-class player on their team, Thierry Henry, as well as Nicolas Anelka, a top striker in goal-scoring form. A moment of brilliance, or a single mistake, could turn the game around.

The second half was only a minute underway when Ireland created another clear chance to score. From a free kick out on the left, Liam Lawrence's strike found its way untouched all the way through to full-back John O'Shea near the far post. He controlled the dropping ball expertly on his chest, but volleyed over from a few yards out. It was not an easy chance, from a challenging angle, but a striker would have expected to score from there, or at least get it on target. But yet again, the French defenders had gone absent without leave.

After 56 minutes, Sidney Govou was brought on to replace the ineffective Gignac. The French began to develop some rhythm and menace, but the Irish defence dealt easily with a few hopeful balls into the penalty area.

Then, one hour into the game, the Irish missed a glorious opportunity to take a two-nil lead. Damien Duff was put through by a measured pass from Robbie Keane. Lloris rushed off his line as Duff prepared to shoot, but Duff's shot with his weaker right foot was slightly deflected by French defender Bacary Sagna making up ground from Duff's right. It was enough to allow Lloris to make the save.

From the counter-attack, some uncertainty in the Irish defence allowed France their first real chance of the game, but Henry found the tight angle and the presence of Dunne and Given too much to overcome and the chance was gone.

Then, within a couple of minutes, Ireland made two substitutions. Darron Gibson replaced Glenn Whelan, and the injured John

O'Shea was replaced by Paul McShane. Again, France began to show signs of some coherence, and Gibson and McShane were soon in the game defending well, deep in the Irish penalty area. But just as the French were starting to apply some sustained pressure, with Given saving from Yoann Gourcuff and Henry heading wide, Ireland was back at the other end threatening to wrap the game up.

Seventy-two minutes had been played when a lovely passing interchange involving Liam Lawrence saw Keane put through at the edge of the six-yard box. He skipped past the advancing Lloris, but his touch was just a little heavy and the ball outran him to roll wide before he could apply a scoring final touch.

The final minutes were played out with no further heart-stopping moments. Florent Malouda replaced Gourcuff with two minutes remaining, so the French had used their three permitted substitutes, with the fans' favourite Karim Benzema still on the bench.

And then came extra time. The Irish had so far performed heroically, but missed several clear-cut opportunities to put the tie beyond France's reach. Most commentators agreed that Ireland had been the better team in regulation time, but how often has it happened that a team which has failed to take advantage of its chances came to rue those misses?

As extra time unfolded, the French began to come to life, with Anelka taking a leading role. After three minutes he sent a long-range effort along the ground but just wide, and four minutes later he broke through the Irish defence on the right. Shay Given advanced, stretching to reach the ball, which Anelka tipped just past him. Anelka went down, and both sides appealed. The French wanted a penalty, the Irish a yellow card for diving. Martin Hansson, the referee, gave a goal kick. The replays suggested the call was probably correct, and a key factor was that Anelka appeared to have already lost control of the ball when he went down.

By this time the French were definitely in the ascendancy, and two minutes later Govou volleyed the ball sweetly into the net from twelve yards out, but the goal was correctly ruled out for offside. It was a close but correct call, but the pressure was clearly increasing on the Irish defence.

Thirteen minutes into extra time came the decisive goal. It was one that would become one of the most famous goals ever in a World Cup qualifying match, but for all the wrong reasons. France was awarded a free kick in midfield, which Malouda floated into a crowded Irish penalty area. The ball was too high for the jumping Dunne and Squillaci, and dropped to the left of the goal. Henry stole in behind McShane, prevented it from going out of play, and crossed for Gallas to head home. It all happened at lightning speed, and most of those at the game would have only appreciated the sequence *free kick – cross – goal*. Hansson signalled a goal, as the French team and fans celebrated wildly. McShane might have done better to deal with the ball before it reached Henry. Given might just possibly have made a move for it once it sailed over the main group in the penalty area (but he likely would have had to be out of position in the first place to do this).

But even before Gallas directed the ball into the net, several Irish defenders had their arms raised in appeal. Shay Given ran immediately to Hansson, and on the touchline Giovanni Trapattoni remonstrated with the fourth official. They were claiming that Henry had handled before crossing.

The video replays left no doubt. Henry's outstretched left arm had prevented the ball going out of play, and then he had raised his left hand to control the ball further before his cross. In addition, the replays showed that both Squillaci and Gallas were offside when the free-kick was taken. However, after a brief consultation with the assistant referee on the far side of the pitch, Hansson confirmed that the goal stood.

Early in the second period of extra time, the Irish made their final substitution, with Aidan McGeady replacing Liam Lawrence. But the Irish seemed to have lost their self-belief and inspiration, and appeared worn-out, physically and mentally. They had nothing more to offer apart from a few hopeful balls into the French penalty area which came to nothing. The final whistle sounded to confirm that France had qualified for the World Cup finals. Ireland was eliminated.

There were some who said that Ireland had only themselves to blame by not being able to convert one or other of the chances they created in the second half. While there is some truth in this, the opportunities that fell to O'Shea and Keane were not "sitters" by any means. Duff's chance was more clear-cut, but not enough credit has been given to the French defence, which did make it as difficult as possible for him. This aside, if a team that creates several good goal-scoring chances in a game but fails to take them does not deserve to win, what does the team that creates little or nothing deserve?

One aspect of the game that has been neglected in the controversy following Henry's handball was the performance of the teams in extra time. France was definitely stronger in this phase of the game. It seemed that the Irish had given everything in regulation time and they did not create a single dangerous threat to the French goal, either before or after Gallas scored. We pointed out that Keane's goal for Ireland followed several minutes of repeated attacks on the French goal. So too did the Gallas goal – coming shortly after two chances for Anelka, and Govou's disallowed strike. Such sustained pressure does create extra problems for defenders, but also places extra pressure on referees. This is particularly true if the officials are faced with the prospect of disallowing the home team a goal for the second time within a few minutes, having also just denied a serious penalty appeal. Indeed, a study of all the psychological factors involved in the French goal would be a major undertaking.

The short half-time break in extra time did not allow time or opportunity for the Irish team to see the replays of Henry's handball. Had it done so, it might just have been the inspiration that the players could have done with to dig deep in that last fifteen minutes and secure the goal that would have sent them through.

Nevertheless, the French fans, the players and the management team on the bench celebrated. The Irish were despondent, many of the players openly in tears. Thierry Henry sat down for a few moments with Richard Dunne, before offering him a consoling hug. The Irish players' disappointment was only to turn to anger later in the dressing room, when they all had the opportunity to see for themselves, over and over again, exactly how France had scored the vital goal.

France: Lloris (Lyon), Sagna (Arsenal), Escudé (Seville), Gallas (Arsenal), Evra (Manchester United), L. Diarra (Real Madrid), A. Diarra (Bordeaux), Anelka (Chelsea), Gourcuff (Bordeaux), Henry (Barcelona), Gignac (Toulouse). Subs: Squillaci (Seville) for Escudé (9 minutes), Govou (Lyon) for Gignac (56 minutes), Malouda (Chelsea) for Gourcuff (88 minutes).

Ireland: Given (Manchester City), O'Shea (Manchester United), St Ledger (Middlesbrough), Dunne (Aston Villa), Kilbane (Hull City), Lawrence (Stoke City), Whelan (Stoke City), Andrews (Blackburn

Rovers), Duff (Fulham), Doyle (Wolverhampton), Keane (Tottenham Hotspur). Subs: Gibson (Manchester United) for Whelan (63 minutes), McShane (Hull City) for O'Shea (66 minutes), McGeady (Glascow Celtic) for Lawrence (107 minutes).

> *My thoughts were for Trapattoni. He had prepared a team magnificently. It was a fantastic performance by them.*
> Alex Ferguson

— 7 —

Reaction

EVEN BEFORE THE ball had crossed the goal line, the nearby Irish defenders had their arms raised and their faces turned towards the referee in appeal. The image of goalkeeper Shay Given chasing after the referee, and the anguish, frustration and pain on his face when he realises that his appeal is falling on deaf ears, will long remain in the memory of Irish football supporters.

In fact, this was such a high-profile game, and its conclusion was so controversial, that opinions were voiced by all and sundry around the globe. The players, Irish and French, obviously would have something to say. But so would other players, former players, football managers, commentators, journalists, football associations, FIFA, spectators, and football supporters from both sides and from around the world. Even philosophers had something to say on the matter. And let us not forget the politicians. Well, on second thoughts, let us perhaps forget what they had to say.

Ireland and Aston Villa defender Richard Dunne did not mince his words. "We were cheated," he said. He implied that the decision to allow the goal was tied in with the seeding for the play-offs, saying, "The people who run the game got exactly what they wanted." In fact, he felt the handball was not difficult to see and should not have even required video replay. He also pointed out the fact that the linesman had missed calling two French players offside when the free kick was taken. Dunne revealed that referee Martin Hansson told him on the field that he was 100% sure that Henry had not handled the ball. We can only presume that Hansson meant he was sure he had not *seen* Henry handle it, which is not quite the same thing. Dunne also reported what Henry said to him after the final whistle. While admitting the handball, he claimed it was unintentional, and that Ireland was undeservedly eliminated. Richard Dunne is a much admired player, both for his playing skills and his commitment to fair play. He was at least able to take some positive things from the game, pointing to Ireland's great performance and the confidence that should carry into future qualifying campaigns. He did not succumb to what must have been a strong temptation to do to Thierry Henry what Eric Cantona might have done to him after the game was over.

Robbie Keane also emphasised the role of the football authorities, singling out UEFA President Michel Platini, and FIFA President Sepp Blatter. "They are all probably clapping hands, Platini sitting up there on the phone to Blatter, probably texting each other," he said angrily. Keane pointed out that the type of instant reaction of the nearby Irish players does not occur without cause. "He almost caught it and ran into the net with it," said a devastated Keane. This is an exaggeration, of course, and if he had done this, we expect that the referee would have spotted it!

John O'Shea was reluctant to say too much, afraid of getting into "trouble", but described the handball as "blatant". Kevin Kilbane saw his last chance of appearing at another World Cup finals disappear, but confirmed that the referee told him during the game that he was 100% correct in ruling that there was no handball. In the *Sunday Times* four days after the game, Kilbane called Henry's assertion to him that he could not help the handball a lie. "He blatantly lied to me by saying it was unavoidable," wrote Kilbane.

Shay Given, as expected given his reaction to the seeding issue, emphasised the role of the football authorities while having no hesitation in describing Ireland as having been cheated out of a place in the finals. Liam Lawrence was just as angry, describing a smirk on Henry's face. Seán St Ledger dismissed Henry's claim of accidental handball, and recalled watching the replay where "you see his eyes looking at the ball, and you see his hand move." But St Ledger touched a sensitive nerve when he went on to say, "If it was one of our players we probably wouldn't have said anything either. If we were going to the World Cup, we wouldn't be talking about TV replays and referees."

Some more provocative comments came from Damien Duff. He stated that FIFA wanted the big teams, including France, in the World Cup and went on, "And, it may sound silly, but they want teams sponsored by adidas. Adidas sponsor the World Cup, they sponsor France." While this may well be true, it is not possible to conclude that referee Hansson or Fredrik Nilsson, his assistant on the far side who missed the offsides and the handball, were directly influenced to the extent that they willingly and deliberately failed to disallow the goal. Adidas spokesman Jon Deacon was not impressed, denying such a conspiracy. Damien Duff is reported to be paid around €100,000 for promoting adidas footwear.

While blaming football's administrators and the officials, Duff was also quick to suggest that Henry had only done what most others might also have done in the circumstances. He said, "If it was down the other end and it was going out of play, I'd have chanced my arm. You can't blame him. He's a clever player but you expect the ref to see it, it was so blatant."

The comments by Seán St Ledger and Damien Duff about Henry's action being part of the reality of football today may well be true. But it is not what the fans go to see. And for these two Irish fans in particular, we personally would not have travelled to South Africa (as we had planned to) to support a team which had cheated its way to the finals.

The incident did happen very quickly, and went unnoticed by most of the spectators present at the match. This explains the reaction of the crowd to the goal, and the French celebrations at the conclusion. It also explains the exceptionally measured response of the Irish players. The true hurt only hit home when the players watched the video replays in the dressing room after the game. Several players describe the mood being transformed from one of deep disappointment to one of deepest anger.

Irish assistant coach Marco Tardelli suggested that if the referee had asked Henry had he handled it, "I think Henry would have said he did." We agree, and at the same time question the possible outcome of such a course of action. Considering what Henry actually did later say, he would likely have responded that yes he did handle it but it was accidental. And the referee, not having seen the incident himself, would have felt justified in allowing the goal. One commentator, picking up on Henry's comment that he was not the referee, bemoaned the fact that he was not. Indeed, had he been, he would have noticed himself handling the ball!

Tony Cascarino was unequivocal. "To me, the handball was pure, calculated cheating. Accidental? He handballed it to keep it in, then slightly knocked it again to get it nicely on his foot." Former Irish manager Mick McCarthy commented on the two offside French players, and said, "You can't see everything when you're a referee," but that the assistant on the touchline should have seen "either the offside or the handball". Niall Quinn saw the incident as "the biggest injustice I have ever seen in sport". RTE's football pundits Johnny Giles and Eamon Dunphy were less critical of Henry, and thought the Irish defense should have done better to prevent the goal.

Ipswich manager Roy Keane added spice to the debate when suggesting that the FAI deserved no less. He criticised Paul McShane for poor marking of Henry in the lead-up to the goal, and Shay Given for not dealing with a ball in his six-yard box. He criticised the Irish team for not being mentally strong enough, pointing to missed goal-scoring chances in both legs of the tie. He did feel the supporters, the manager, and some of the players deserved better. However, he had little sympathy for the FAI. Strangely reminiscent of the vengeful attitude of Henry after being the victim of a poor refereeing decision in a Champions League game, Keane said, "What goes around comes around." Roy Keane later apologised to Irish supporters for his "over the top" comments.

The Irish newspapers reacted as expected to the latest national tragedy. They carried detailed match reports, interviews and analysis, and screamed headlines like "Armed Robbery". Underneath the anger and frustration there was a definite tone of tremendous pride in the unexpected quality of the Irish performance, and the admirable manner with which the players reacted to their undeserved elimination. The British press had a similar reaction, their headline writers vying with each other to see which paper could provide the headline most typical of their particular journalistic style of indignation. Readers will immediately recognise that it was not the *Guardian* which carried the headline "French Nickers" and that the *Mirror* did not lead with "Irish hopes crushed as Thierry Henry hands victory to France". With a large Irish community in the UK, and most of the team members playing in the English Premier League, the media there tend to have a very supportive attitude towards the Irish team. Nonetheless, these attitudes are not reciprocated in Ireland, where traditionally fans support England's opponents.

The Irish were still gripped by World Cup fever in June 2010, and cheered loudly for whoever played against France. Advertisers sought to exploit the mood with offers of free pizzas for every goal scored against France, and free beer and discounts upon France's elimination. It is a measure of the depth of passionate feelings aroused by the manner of French qualification that if England and France had met in the World Cup finals, the Irish would, possibly for the first time in history, have supported the English.

One of the more intriguing aspects of the media coverage was to be found in the letters pages of the Irish papers. So very many of those who wrote in were French supporters embarrassed by, and apologetic for, the undeserved victory.

The French reaction was overwhelmingly one of embarrassment. There were two reasons for this. One was the manner in which they had qualified. The second was the poor standard of the French performance. Bixente Lizarazu described the French performance as "catastrophic", and *Le Monde* referred to "one of their most impoverished and indigestible games".

The French state TV channel *France 2* carried out an online poll after the game. The response showed that 88% felt that Henry was wrong to have handled the ball, 81% felt that qualification was undeserved, and 71% felt that Raymond Domenech should be sacked. Contrast this with Domenech's view that "everyone who loves the French team is pleased with this qualification".

The French newspaper *Le Monde* conducted an online poll asking readers whether France deserved to go to the World Cup finals. The "non" choice received 88% of votes. We suppose that did leave enough supporters willing to share Raymond Domenech's "happiness" at France's qualification. The French sports teachers' union SNEP-FSU saw the incident for what it was, and condemned Henry's handball as an act of "indisputable cheating". The union also directly criticised Raymond Domenech and some of the players for upholding the philosophy that the end justifies the means. Thierry Roland, described by *The Times* as the doyen of French TV football commentators, said, "It's a scandal, a shame with a capital S." Echoing the French response to the 9/11 attacks on New York, Jacques Attali (an economist and former aide to President Mitterand) said "Nous sommes tous Irlandais." (On 12th September 2001, the *Le Monde* headline read: "Nous sommes tous Américains".) *Le Parisien* widened the theme, saying, "The handball of Henry has brought a decisive contribution to the theme 'being French is being ashamed of one's national team'." Yves Rimet, grandson of Jules Rimet, the Frenchman who founded the World Cup, said, "The ethics of sport were flouted."

The French players' reactions were notable for their lack of remorse, closing ranks around their captain. Manchester United defender Patrice Evra said in *L'Equipe* that the French should erect a statue to Henry. Well, perhaps they will. Statues have after all been erected in honour of lesser men than Thierry Henry. While Evra considered it fair that the world press should criticise Henry, he complained of the French doing the same. Evra said that Henry would have betrayed his teammates if he had admitted right away to the referee that he had handled. It appears not to have occurred to Evra that Henry might just have betrayed the very game that brought them both fame and fortune.

Sébastien Squillaci typified the French players' reaction when he said, "It's part of the game, it played in our favour tonight, maybe some other time it will play against us." He went on to say, "We're competitors and we're there to win. The goal may not be valid but we'll take it."

David Ginola expressed embarrassment and a distinct lack of pride, describing the outcome as "pure injustice". Eric Cantona was shocked by Henry going to sit beside Dunne and consoling him, saying, "If I'd been Irish he wouldn't have lasted three seconds." Another French philosopher, Alain Finkeilkraut, commented that "From the moral point of view, I would almost have preferred a defeat for France." Why only *almost*?

The Italian press reaction to the French qualification was more emotional than analytical. The Italians do not try to hide their support for the Irish team managed by one of Italy's favourite football icons, Giovanni Trapattoni. *Corriere Dello Sport's* front page read simply: "France, What A Scandal!" *Gazzetta Dello Sport* called it a "vile" goal, and supported the introduction of video replay for referees. Many Italian papers were reminded of Italy's exit from the 2002 World Cup, and the role that questionable refereeing played in that exit. "Another Moreno, another World Cup scandal..." Football people have long memories.

At the time of the Paris match, Thierry Henry played his club football with Barcelona. There is a lot of history behind this particular marriage. After the Champions League final in 2006, when Arsenal lost to Barcelona, Henry committed himself to staying at Arsenal. He complained about the attention he received from Barcelona defender Carles Puyol, saying after the game, "Next time I'll learn to dive maybe." At the World Cup finals in Germany in 2006, his theatrics after striving with Spain's Puyol for the ball

(Henry went down dramatically, his hands covering his face) earned Puyol a yellow card. From the resultant free kick, France scored and Spain was on its way out of the World Cup. In 2007 Henry was transferred to Barcelona, where he plays on the same team as Puyol.

Naturally, the Spanish press had a lot to say about Henry's handball. An editorial in *Marca*, Spain's best-selling newspaper, called for a replay in the interests of justice. The sports paper *AS* focused on the referee, and the ease with which big decisions tend to favour certain teams. The Catalan *Sport* joked of Henry having a hand injury treated on his return to Barcelona. Pep Guardiola, manager of Barcelona, excused Henry's unintentional "reaction", but said that he should not be proud of what he did. He supported calls for using video replay for major decisions.

The *Japan Times* described France qualifying for the finals "with help from Swedish referee Martin Hansson", and called it "a shameful incident" which will "brand Henry for life". The *Sydney Morning Herald* described it as a "day of infamy", saying that "France cheated their way on to the last flight to South Africa." Also from Australia, the *Daily Telegraph* provided a much more measured response: "Henry outplayed some of the greatest scammers, hoaxers, matchfixers, ball-tamperers and blatant rule-benders to earn a place in infamy as one of the biggest cheats in world sport." Johannesburg's *Mail & Guardian* commented on Henry damaging his reputation, and what it says about modern football. "That such a talent, such a modern superstar had to resort to such a blatant act of deceit shows where the game is today." The *Buenos Aires Herald*, in a piece entitled "Infamous Goal" pointed out that Henry was now being compared to Maradona, but not in a way he would have wished. It also highlighted the ongoing French criticism of manager Domenech after a very poor French performance.

Soccer, as football is called in North America, has never really gripped the sporting public in the New World as it has on the rest of the planet. What happened in Paris on 18th November will certainly not help change that. In the USA, it must compete with hockey, football (the American kind), basketball and baseball. All of these sports have embraced technology to try to ensure that fair and correct decisions are made during the game. Sports fans there find it simply incredible that in this day and age an incident like the handball can go undetected and unpunished, and that the offending team can claim a major reward as a result of such unfair play.

Writing on the *New England Sports Network* on 19th November 2009, Adam Hirshfield tried to explain to sports fans what had happened in a sport they normally do not take much notice of.

Imagine the Celtics losing Game 7 of the NBA finals on a last-second layin by Kobe Bryant after he takes the ball at halfcourt and runs — without dribbling, mind you — to the hoop for the score. Two hours after you undergo root-canal surgery.

It would be like ex-umpire Don Denkinger missing a clear play at first base on which the Red Sox' game-winning run would have scored. In Game 7 of the ALCS. Against the Yankees. On your birthday.

Picture referee Ed Hochuli prematurely blowing his whistle on a legit game-winning fumble return by the Patriots in the AFC championship game. Then he punches you in the stomach on his way off the field.

Time magazine listed Henry's handball as number two on its list of "Top Ten Sporting Cheats". In first place came baseball's Mark McGwire, who admitted using performance-enhancing drugs during his home run record season in 1998. Maradona's "hand of God" goal was listed a distant tenth on the list.

Not everyone was quite so quick to criticise Henry. Arsène Wenger can claim as much responsibility as anyone for Henry's climb to the top of world football. He managed Henry at Monaco and during his spectacular career at Arsenal. While admitting his embarrassment as a Frenchman, Wenger was slow to criticise Henry for the incident. He cited his years of fair play, and criticised the French Football Federation for failing to support the player by ignoring calls for a replay.

Lionel Messi, arguably the best player in the world today, also found words to support his Barcelona teammate Henry. Describing what happened as "just an incident during a game of football", he felt Henry had done the right thing in apologising. But then what else could he say? Messi himself scored a goal with his hand (Maradona-style) playing for Barcelona against Espanyol in 2007. Furthermore, we doubt if he would have the same attitude had such an "incident" prevented Argentina from qualifying for the World Cup finals. Similarly David Beckham defended Henry, calling what happened an "accident". Zinedine Zidane was also prepared to defend Henry, saying he was not a cheat, and that the handball was an error, "a simple match fact" and part of the game. Brazilian legend Pelé also excused Henry for the "accident" while satisfying his Irish interviewers with praise for the Irish performance and calling the result unfair. He thought that such incidents were more typical of the South American game than the way Europeans play. None of these players chose to comment on Henry's goal celebration, which was not instinctive, did not occur in a fraction of a second, and could hardly be labelled an "accident".

It is interesting that the word "cheat" carries with it such a severe moral implication. When we look at the dictionary definition, it is a much more benign word.

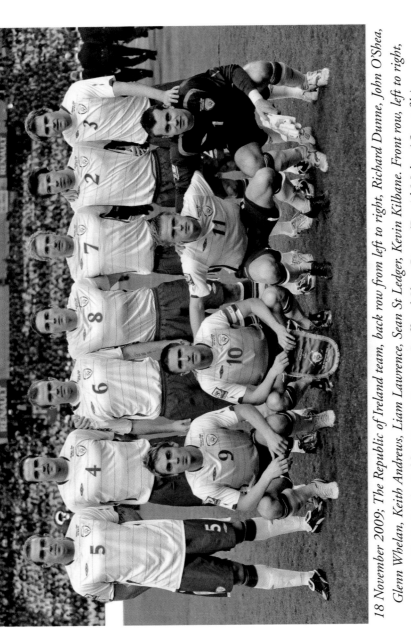

18 November 2009: The Republic of Ireland team, back row from left to right, Richard Dunne, John O'Shea, Glenn Whelan, Keith Andrews, Liam Lawrence, Sean St Ledger, Kevin Kilbane. Front row, left to right, Kevin Doyle, Robbie Keane, Damien Duff and Shay Given (David Maher / Sportsfile)

The best fans in the world. (Stephen McCarthy / Sportsfile)

William Gallas scores. Referee Martin Hansson watches from a distance. (David Maher / Sportsfile)

Celebration on the terraces as the Irish plead in vain. (David Maher / Sportsfile)

Irish fans react to Hansson awarding France's goal. (Alan Betson/ The Irish Times)

Damien Duff after the final whistle. (David Maher / Sportsfile)

Thierry Henry admits his handball to Richard Dunne.
(Stephen McCarthy / Sportsfile)

Thierry Henry embraces Richard Dunne after the game, but Dunne seems a little less enthusiastic. (Stephen McCarthy / Sportsfile)

Raymond Domenech. He was puzzled that French fans were not as happy with qualification as he was. (David Maher / Sportsfile)

Ireland's favourite Italian, Giovanni Trapattoni.
(Brian Lawless / Sportsfile)

According to the *Compact Oxford English Dictionary* there are three ways to define the meaning of the verb "to cheat":

1. act dishonestly or unfairly in order to gain an advantage.
2. deprive of something by deceitful or unfair means.
3. avoid (something undesirable) by luck or skill: *she cheated death in a spectacular crash.*

Choose whichever definition you like, but in fact according to all three interpretations, Thierry Henry cheated when he handled the ball. Perhaps he did not with the first handball, but most clearly he did with the second one. He acted unfairly to gain an advantage, he thus deprived Ireland by unfair means, and he certainly avoided something undesirable for his team. In addition, he was skilful in how he controlled the ball with first his arm, and then his hand in quick succession. And finally, he can count himself lucky that he was not caught.

Context is hugely important, and it explains why Henry's handball became the subject of so much debate. Had France been leading 2–0 in normal time, and had a similar goal been scored, it would have received only passing notice. But the goal decided who would progress to the finals of the World Cup – the greatest sporting event on the planet. In addition, the goal eliminated an Irish team which embodied all the best sporting attributes of the underdog. They produced a superb, even heroic, performance against all the odds, when their chances had already been written off. This was the stuff of our sporting fantasies. This was a dream coming true. This was that last-minute goal we scored, or imagined we scored, at nine years of age into a goal made of two schoolbags, to win the World Cup for Ireland, or Brazil, or France. And suddenly, it was gone.

There were two further aspects of the background to this goal which resulted in the incident gaining the widespread attention that it did. One was Thierry Henry's stature in the game. He was not only a French international player, but he was a true superstar, known and recognised around the world. And finally, the offence was a hand-ball, in a football match. In fact, the most prominent rule in association football that distinguishes it from all other major ball games is the rule against handling.

In conclusion, it seems that most sports people who voiced their opinions thought that Thierry Henry had cheated. As things stand, the sport's rules allow such cheating to go undetected and unpunished. So, if we accept a fair verdict of cheating, it seems we can conclude that cheating has become an integral part of the game. While this is true, it remains, in our opinion, unacceptable. And the responsibility for allowing this situation to continue in the sport rests squarely on FIFA, whose refusal to introduce reliable, visible and effective measures to detect and punish such incidents is almost incomprehensible.

Some people excused Henry's actions, as he was to do himself, as an instinctive part of the game. Interestingly, many who held this opinion were either players or former players. The higher the profile of the players, the less interested they appeared to be in criticising Henry. This is understandable when you consider that their successes have been achieved in the current football culture.

However, before you move on to the next chapter we suggest you take a few moments in absolute silence, undisturbed, and try to really, seriously imagine how you yourself, and the football world, would have reacted had it been Robbie Keane who had hand-passed to Richard Dunne for the game winner.

Finally, it must be emphasised that the Irish supporters' behaviour after such a crushing blow was exemplary. It is not for nothing that they are considered the best fans in the world. They were missed at the finals.

"What is the use of a book," thought Alice, *"without pictures or conversation?"*
Lewis Carroll (*Alice's Adventures in Wonderland*)

— 8 —

Replay – no way

After France's controversial qualification for the World Cup finals, the Football Association of Ireland (FAI) petitioned FIFA for the game to be replayed. It came as no surprise that FIFA refused. The French Football Federation (FFF) then refused to consider a direct appeal from the FAI for a replay, even though Thierry Henry belatedly supported this proposal. Henry's statement, issued on Friday 20th November, described a replay as "the fairest solution". He was criticised for only making this call after FIFA had already ruled against a replay.

Considering all possible outcomes and impacts, the FAI shouldn't have asked for a replay, and FIFA were right to refuse. In the interest of clearing the names of its team, manager, and captain, however, the FFF should have agreed to a replay. Had they done so, France would have had an excellent chance of prevailing, and could have gone to the World Cup finals, heads held high, and with the backing of their own fans and football supporters everywhere.

John Delaney is the chief executive of the FAI. He submitted a formal request to FIFA for the game to be replayed in the interests of justice and fair play. "Every time I go to a FIFA conference, I hear all about fair play and integrity," he said. He emphasised the world-wide audience the game had attracted.

The FAI claimed a precedent for such an action. In 2005, a play-off World Cup qualifying game between Uzbekistan and Bahrain was ordered to be replayed. Uzbekistan had been awarded a penalty from which they scored. However, the referee disallowed the goal and gave Bahrain a free kick because an Uzbekistan player had encroached in the penalty area when the kick was taken. He should have ordered the kick to be retaken. FIFA claimed a replay was justified on this occasion because the rules of the game were not applied. This is hardly a unique argument. Every time a goal is scored from a player who is offside, and allowed to stand, the rules of the game are not applied.

This story had an unexpected final twist to it, which received little attention when it was mentioned in the context of the FAI's appeal. Uzbekistan had won the original game 1–0, but demanded a 3–0 forfeit. Instead FIFA ordered a replay. The replayed game finished 1–1, and the second leg in Bahrain ended 0–0. In the end, Bahrain progressed on away goals.

In 1999, Arsenal and Sheffield United played in the fifth round of the FA Cup, with Arsenal winning 2–1. Arsenal scored their winning goal after an attack following a throw-in, which they were expected to return to the opposition because it had been conceded to allow treatment for an injured player. Arsenal, under manager Arsène Wenger, graciously agreed to a replay, which they again won 2–1. This game provided some precedent for a game to be replayed when both teams agreed. More recently, just one month before the France–Ireland match, Sunderland defeated Liverpool 1–0 in the English Premier League. The winning goal was scored when a shot deflected past the Liverpool goalkeeper off a beach ball thrown on to the pitch. The goal should have been disallowed and play restarted with a drop-ball. Here too, the rules of the game were not applied. However, no request was made to have the game replayed.

Support for the Ireland-France game to be replayed came from many sources. Irish politicians found a new cause to support, vying to outshine each other in their commitment to the cause, their ethical pronouncements, and their opportunistic patriotism. More significantly, over 500,000 people signed an online petition. Many embarrassed French supporters wanted a replay. Arsène Wenger questioned the credibility of France going to the World Cup under these circumstances, and joined those calling for the game to be replayed. But the majority of those professionally involved in football did not think a replay was feasible. Irish manager Giovanni Trapattoni conceded that it was "impossible".

FIFA responded as expected. "There is no way the game can be replayed. To do so would cause absolute chaos for football." So instead of absolute chaos, we have to settle for simple chaos. Let us imagine for a moment that the game was replayed, and the replay was decided by a goal scored by a player who was clearly offside, or by some other kind of refereeing error. Under the current guidelines, officials would not be allowed to use any different means to help them make better decisions. There would be a real possibility of such a thing happening. Then we would indeed have absolute chaos.

FIFA directed attention to Law 5: "The referee has full authority to enforce the Laws of the Game in connection with the match to which he has been appointed and that the decisions of the referee regarding facts connected with play are final." FIFA does seem to have a creative interpretation of some English words. If the referee gets the "facts" wrong, then they are not "facts", but misinterpretations of events. It must also be pointed out that Law 5 leaves referees potentially wide open to corruption and bribery, because it states essentially that a referee is right, even when he is wrong. How can a referee be deemed to have enforced the Laws of the Game when his decisions are incorrect? Furthermore, once a decision has been made, there is no going back. Can you imagine the following scenario? The referee of a future World Cup final is found guilty in a court of law of accepting a bribe to influence the result. Yet the bribe achieves its aim because his decisions, however wrong or corrupt, are final. While replaying games would not be an ideal norm, FIFA needs to do more to ensure that referees are enabled to make better decisions, and that the process is both transparent and reproducible. Video replay technology fits these criteria. Accepting "errors" as "facts" is absurd and unfair. Such a situation will always leave FIFA open to allegations of favouritism and corruption. In many sports, teams and individuals who cheat risk disqualification. Even in the less than pristine world of the Olympic Games, athletes who have cheated have been stripped of titles, records and medals. This has even been done retrospectively, and without absolute chaos.

Having failed to convince FIFA to order a replay, the FAI was then hopeful that the FFF would offer to replay the game. However, the FFF held firm, accepting World Cup qualification regardless of the manner in which it was achieved. After the game, FFF president Jean Pierre Escalettes had stated: "I am really happy and I share the great success with the players on the pitch. We have had refereeing mistakes against us in this qualification campaign." These are hardly the words of someone likely to support calls for the game to be replayed. The FFF referred to FIFA's decision to refuse a replay. An FFF spokesperson said, "FIFA is the ruler of the game and we have to abide by what they say."

The French refusal statement was noteworthy in another respect.

It perpetuated the mistaken idea that miscarriages of justice in sport should be accepted and will even out in time. This "what goes around comes around" attitude is hardly the way forward. In expressing sympathy with the disappointment and bitterness of the Irish, the FFF claimed a special understanding "because French football has suffered events of a similar nature in the past". According to this philosophy, international sport should accept cheating because everyone involved has equal opportunity to cheat and be cheated. The FFF offered its "full support" to Henry, recognising his honesty in admitting the handball, and the pressures he was under. It failed to point out that his "honesty" was delayed long enough to make no difference, and that he brought the pressures upon himself by his own actions.

The *Sunday Independent* carried a story on 22nd November 2009 claiming that French manager Raymond Domenech was the sole obstacle to the FFF agreeing to replay the game. The article claimed that he prevailed over the wishes of the majority of the French squad, the French public, and key federation officials. It also claimed that FIFA was willing to sanction a replay if the French agreed. The source for these claims was not revealed. Nevertheless, Domenech had already made it clear he had no guilty feelings about qualification. "For me, it's a game incident and not cheating. Therefore I don't see why we are asked to apologise."

Football authorities found themselves in a strange position after the game. The FAI could not simply ignore what had happened without making some sort of protest. FIFA would have been content to remain silent, but had no great difficulty pointing to the rulebook in response to whatever form the Irish protest took. In some ways, the greatest pressure was on the FFF, and that pressure was mostly coming from the French public, through the media, as they overwhelmingly expressed their embarrassment at how qualification was achieved.

The FAI knew after the game that the Irish team had been cheated of a chance at qualification, but it had no legitimate way of correcting the situation. The appeal for a replay was made as a "we must do something" reaction. They searched for a precedent and found one. But their appeal was more in hope than in expectation.

Would a replay have been a fair solution? Irish assistant coach Liam Brady said, "We would go to Paris and play the match again. I don't think it would come to that, but we'd be willing to play it again in Paris, on their home ground, and have a fair winner."

A replay would have been better than elimination, but it would not have been fair. France would have started with the same advantage they had at the beginning of the Paris leg – a 1–0 lead with an away goal. The great Irish performance in Paris beating France 1–0 in regular time would have been wiped out, deleted, removed from the record. The Irish would begin a goal down and have to do it all over again – unfair, even unjust.

Replay: to play (a match) again

Play-off: an additional match played to decide the outcome of a contest

Oxford English Dictionary

The FAI should have requested a play-off game at a neutral venue (if one could be found, given the passions this game had aroused), not a replay. The outcome of the appeal would have been the same, and FIFA and the FFF would have refused. But by asking for a replay the FAI left itself open to a great danger. That danger was that France would accept the request.

And that is exactly what the French should have done. If the game had been replayed, France could expect a much improved performance from the Paris game. Ireland would be very unlikely to have produced such a high standard of play the second time around. In summary, France would not play so badly again, nor Ireland so well. France would, in all likelihood, have won. The French would have been applauded around the world for their sportsmanship, Thierry Henry could hold his head up again as a sportsman of stature, and the French team would have regained much of the public's support. But there was a risk. So it was not ethics, or rules, or anything else that prevented Domenech's team from replaying the match. It was simply fear – the fear of losing. Judging by their subsequent performance in South Africa, the French had every reason to be fearful.

FAI: Play it again FIFA.
FIFA: We don't think we can....
FAI: You replayed it for Uzbekistan, you can re-play it for us!

— 9 —

Chalk and cheese — two luxury coaches

WHEN IRELAND AND France were paired in the play-offs to qualify for World Cup 2010, sports commentators suggested that France held the upper hand in all respects but two – Ireland was considered to have a better goalkeeper, and a better coach. It was initially understandable why they might come to this conclusion about the respective merits of France's Raymond Domenech and Ireland's Giovanni Trapattoni. But does this view hold up to close scrutiny? After all, Domenech had guided France to a runners-up spot in the 2006 World Cup, and Trapattoni's international coaching record was more notable for its failures than its successes.

Trapattoni – football's passionate philosopher

Giovanni Trapattoni is one of football's iconic managers. While his managerial career is littered with successes, it is ironic that he will likely now be most remembered internationally because of his association with two spectacular failures: Italy's controversial loss to Korea in the 2002 World Cup quarter-finals, and Ireland's elimination from the 2010 World Cup by France.

On a lighter note, he is remembered across Europe for his famous press conference rant in 1998 after a poor Bayern Munich performance, during which he referred to some of his underperforming players as having played like "empty bottles". This passionate attack on his own team, in brutal German, remains accessible online, and has to be seen to be believed (and appreciated), and can only be described to true sporting fans as priceless!

Trapattoni was born on St Patrick's Day 1939, and is the elder statesman of a quartet of Italian managers currently in key posts in European football: Fabio Capello (born 1946, English national team manager), Marcello Lippi (born 1948, two-time Italian national team manager), and Carlo Ancelotti (born 1959, Chelsea manager). Trapattoni was a defensive midfielder of high quality for a Milan team in the late 1950s and early 1960s which won two European Cups (now Champions League). He played 17 times for Italy. He had the reputation of being the most effective marker of the young Pelé, and his shutting down of Eusebio in the 1963 European Cup final played a key role in Milan's 2–1 victory. His exceptional managerial career was highlighted by guiding Juventus to six Italian Championship triumphs (and one European Cup in 1985 – winning the ill-fated final against Liverpool at the Heysel stadium) when he managed them from 1976–1986. He also coached teams to league titles in Germany, Portugal and Austria.

He was in charge of the Italian national team at the World Cup in 2002, and at the European Championships in 2004 – without success. Two years after he was replaced, Italy was once again the winner of the World Cup.

Ireland lured Trapattoni from his position at Red Bull Salzburg in February 2008 with a reported sweetener of about one million euro provided by millionaire businessman Denis O'Brien.

Trapattoni's appointment was greeted with overwhelming approval in Ireland. "Ireland and Giovanni Trapattoni! It's a bit like the resigned and solitary bachelor walking into his local pub with Jennifer Lopez on his arm. Mouths drop open," wrote Keith Duggan in *The Irish Times*. "Il Trap" took over on 1st May 2008 and steadied a very wobbly Irish international team, leading them to an undefeated second place in their World Cup qualifying group, which included world champions Italy, and Bulgaria. He is generally viewed as an intelligent, analytical, but cautious manager. He has been labelled "defensive Trap", and is considered one of the masters of the Italian *catennacio* style. He believes in discipline, and emphasises repetition in practice to reinforce key ideas. He has a philosophical approach to some of the issues the game throws up, and together with a patchy talent for languages, this often results in very entertaining press conferences.

He doesn't always get it right, of course. In this sport, who does? After the 2–2 draw between Ireland and Italy in Dublin in the qualifiers, when Ireland scored late but gave up an even later equalizer, he said that this wouldn't have happened to Italy. In fact it had happened earlier in the Italian home tie, when Ireland was the team to score a late equalizer. And something similar had cost Trap his Italian manager's job when Italy gave up a late equalizer to Sweden at Euro 2004, after Trapattoni had replaced two forwards with two midfielders while leading 1–0.

Trapattoni's response to the defeat to France was pragmatic and measured. On the sidelines at the time he clearly remonstrated with the fourth official about the handball. Somewhat kindly, he refused afterwards to single out Henry himself for criticism. Instead he focused on the referee, asking what criteria were used to choose referees for such important games. He reminded the press of his previous critical encounter with refereeing controversy – Byron Moreno's officiating of the Italy-Korea game at the 2002 World Cup finals. Although Moreno's handling of that game was defended by FIFA and Sepp Blatter, within one year of the finals Moreno had been suspended twice in his native Ecuador, and had retired from refereeing. But a full analysis of the events of that game would merit a book on its own – player injuries, missed chances, a disallowed goal, a red card, a controversial penalty, and a questionable substitution all played a role.

The FAI's appeal to FIFA for the game to be replayed did not excite Trapattoni too much. He knew this was "impossible", but he pointed out correctly that such things can easily happen again unless something is done. In common with most professional managers and players in the game today, he supports the introduction of video technology to decide crucial moments in the game. His opinion is that many of the game's ills can be traced to special interests, and ultimately greed and money. True to his tendency to analyse and think things through, he also questioned the playing of extra time in such two-legged fixtures, as it effectively gives one team an extra 30 minutes of home advantage in the event of a tie. This advantage is hardly offset by the other team having thirty extra minutes to score an away goal.

Certainly Trapattoni emerges from the mayhem with his reputation enhanced, not only for the dignity with which he handled himself in his responses to what had occurred, but also for the manner in which he coached the Irish team to such a great performance.

Perhaps more than most, Trapattoni was one of the first of those involved with the Irish team to begin to "recover" from the trauma of the manner of Ireland's exit, saying: "Sometimes football lets you down but like life it gives you another opportunity every day . . . it's football, it's life." But maybe this is largely because he has the experience of having been there before.

Giovanni Trapattoni has always been ready to engage with the football press. This has resulted in some memorable quotes over the years.

I always say that, in addition to being a coach, I'm also a priest. I go to each player's room and say who is playing and who isn't. I talk and explain. It's a little like confession.
... during Euro 2004, when he was manager of Italy

Don't say cat if you haven't got it in the bag.
... the interpretation here depends on the reader

There will have to be a bubonic plague for me to pick di Canio.
... on whether he might pick Paulo di Canio for Italy in 2000, having fallen out with him at Juventus in 1993

A beautiful game is for 24 hours in the newspapers; a result stands forever.
Raymond Domenech might have said this, but didn't

... with three free-kicks and a corner.
... describing how Greece won the European Championship in 2004

We can learn from Athlone.
Trapattoni was a member of the coaching staff of the AC Milan team which could only draw at Athlone in the UEFA Cup in 1975. Athlone missed a penalty in their home game which finished 0–0, and held Milan scoreless until the 63rd minute of the second leg – but eventually lost 3–0.

The second fiddle doesn't demand to play first fiddle just before a concert.
... describing the main difference between an orchestra conductor and a football manager

Yes, he is built like a wardrobe.
... trying to compliment Richard Dunne after Ireland's home win against Cyprus in the qualifiers

Italy have silk, whereas I only have cotton.
... on the differences between the Irish and Italian squads

With silk you can make a tie, with cotton you can make a shirt.
... a failed attempt to invent a simpler alternative to "paper-rock-scissors"

My feeling now is it would be better for Ireland to play away first ... I don't want to meet another Moreno.
... expressing his hopes for the play-offs on 16th October 2009

Raymond Domenech – one goal in mind

Despite leading a relatively unfancied French team to the World Cup final in 2006, where they lost only on penalties to Italy, Raymond Domenech is an unpopular coach. Why is that so?

Born on 24th January 1952 in Lyon, Domenech was appointed manager of the French national team in 2004 after France's disappointing performance at the European Championship finals in Portugal. Greece, the eventual winners, had eliminated France in the quarter-finals. Four years later, Domenech was retained despite a much worse performance at Euro 2008.

Domenech's twenty-year club career (playing full-back) in the 1970s and 1980s was confined to the French league, playing mostly for Olympique Lyon and later Strasburg. He won a French league title with Strasburg in 1979, in a team which also included Arsène Wenger in midfield. He was capped eight times for France, and returned to coach Lyon from 1989 to 1993 without great success. He then served as manager of the French under-21 team

(1993–2004). His team (which included Thierry Henry, Nicholas Anelka and William Gallas) notably failed to qualify for the Sydney Olympics, losing out 3–2 on aggregate to Italy in 1999. The Italians were coached by Marco Tardelli, and Domenech subsequently accused Italy of bribing the referee. He was fined for making these accusations.

Many of Domenech's squad selections have been subject to criticism, particularly in the run-up to the 2006 World Cup finals. Nevertheless, he managed to salvage a poor qualification campaign after Zinedine Zidane, Claude Makélélé and Lilian Thuram returned from retirement. The key game in this qualification group proved to be a 1–0 victory for France over Ireland in Dublin, the goal being scored by Thierry Henry. Domenech was subsequently criticised for omitting Barcelona and Arsenal wingers Ludovic Giuly and Robert Pires from the squad for the finals. He did include a then-uncapped Franck Ribéry. This decision was later partly justified by Ribéry's performances in Germany and his development into one of Europe's most exciting strikers. Years later, Domenech's selection of 22-year-old Yoann Gourcuff for his first full international in a crucial qualifier against Serbia also was very successful.

France were unimpressive in the group stages in Germany 2006, but came alive after that – defeating Spain, Brazil and Portugal before losing to Italy in a final mostly remembered for Zidane's head-butting offence on Marco Materazzi. Domenech complained that the fourth official had illegally used video evidence to make the call, a claim denied by FIFA. By contrast, most football fans, and even Zidane himself, accepted the red card as an appropriate punishment for the offence. Interestingly, the fourth official who made the call was Spaniard Luis Medina Cantalejo, who was much criticised earlier in the same tournament for his injury-time penalty award to Italy against Australia. Had video replay evidence been used then, Italy might not have gone on to win the World Cup!

Many people expected a new French manager after France's appalling performance at Euro 2008, where they finished last in their group, losing to Italy and the Netherlands, and getting their only point from a scoreless draw with Romania. But the FFF kept him in charge. In the merry-go-round that defines top level coaching, where for example the average duration of a manager's job in the English Premier League is measured in months rather than years, Domenech has received repeated and enviable backing from the FFF. In fact he was in charge of the French national team for more games than any other manager. Domenech has the worst win percentage record of any French manager since 1988 (Table 4).

There are several possible explanations for Domenech's unpopularity among French fans and the French football press. He has often failed to explain his controversial squad choices, and his game strategies have frequently left supporters, commentators, and possibly even his players bewildered. He has been suspected of allowing his interests outside the game to determine some of his coaching decisions, after admitting that he has used tarot cards to try to find out more about his players. However, every manager brings his own personality and preferences to his job. Domenech has claimed (or joked?): "I am not superstitious – it brings bad luck." He has an unimpressive winning record in his playing and coaching career. Significantly, his French team, with a host of quality players to choose from, often performs very poorly. Indeed, many seem to believe that when France does play well, it is in spite of their manager rather than because of him. Prior to the play-off tie with Ireland, French sports paper *L'Equipe* described Domenech as Ireland's best hope to qualify.

Domenech's response to the manner of France's qualification for the 2010 World Cup did not enhance his popularity. While most French supporters and commentators felt at least a sense of guilt, if not outright shame, at cheating their way to qualification, Domenech apparently had no such tender feelings. Amazingly, he expressed his disappointment that the controversy prevented him from fully enjoying France's qualification. In a radio discussion with Bixente Lizarazu a few hours after the game, he would not discuss France's poor performance. The exchanges became quite heated, as Domenech repeatedly refused to talk about the game, saying, "No, tonight we don't ask ourselves anything, we're just happy because we're qualified." He was quoted afterwards as saying that he didn't "see what we could have done better". The millions of people who watched the game could well have told him – France could have played much better (even just well), and they might have progressed by means of a legitimate goal. His comment on Henry's goal focused on the fact that he himself did not see the handball, and the undeniable fact that the referee awarded the goal. He described the result as "miraculous".

Calls for Domenech's replacement as French manager were renewed after France's inept performance against Ireland in Paris. However, the FFF continued to support him – a spokesperson claiming that when you win "you don't change the coach". This prompts the very obvious question as to why he was not replaced after Euro 2008. True, Domenech managed to deflect some attention from the team's performance then by proposing to his girlfriend live on TV after France's exit. Consistent with his views that results may be determined by various non-footballing influences, he complained that "the layout of the hotel was all wrong". Former French manager Aimé Jacquet (under whose watch the French team did win a World Cup) thought Domenech should have been sacked after Euro 2008, and bemoaned the current French "team's playing style or,

Table 4. French national team managers' records since 1988

Manager	Year	P	W	D	L	%*
Michel Platini	1988–1992	29	16	8	5	55.2
Gerard Houllier	1992–1993	12	7	1	4	58.3
Aimé Jacquet	1994–1998	53	34	16	3	64.2
Roger Lemerre	1998–2002	53	34	11	8	64.2
Jacques Santini	2002–2004	28	22	4	2	78.6
Raymond Domenech	2004–2010	79	41	24	14	51.9

*Percentage of games won

rather, the lack of it". Xavier Rivoire of *France Football* magazine accused Domenech of having no plan from the very beginning of their qualifying campaign for South Africa 2010.

Raymond Domenech is not noted for his sense of humour. After Eric Cantona described him as "the worst coach in French football since Louis XVI", he responded that Louis XVI was not a coach. Strange but true. When Catherine Ringer had a viral hit in 2009 with "Je Kiffe Raymond" ("I fancy Raymond") – including the immortal lyrics "if he attacked my penalty areas, I would be without defenders" – he appeared unsure as to whether the song was a compliment or an insult. His public relations advisor Franck Hocquemiller thought it was "very positive". How many football managers have a public relations advisor? How many need one? FFF president Jean-Pierre Escalettes apparently thought Domenech did, once referring to the manager's media relations as "at times disastrous".

Indeed, it is hard to define what Domenech's exact influence on France's tactics and strategy has been. The French under Domenech have been inconsistent. There is no clear pattern. His greatest contribution to French football may well have been to welcome Zidane back from retirement for the 2006 World Cup qualifiers and finals. In the light of where this led, even Zidane himself may now think it might have been better if he had simply said, "Non, merci."

Domenech's attitude that the manner of victory is less important than the result itself is not shared by the majority of football fans. The reaction to what happened on 18th November provides strong evidence that followers of football do care very strongly about how a victory is achieved, regardless of whether their team benefits or not. Football is a sport, and people want and expect fair play. Winning through cheating is unacceptable in football, as in any sport. For most of us, we do not believe that the end justifies the means.

So France qualified for the finals, and Domenech remained as unpopular as ever with the French. We believe this is partly because he is perceived as not being skilled enough for the job he holds, but perhaps even more so because his sporting philosophy is so different from that of many millions of football fans.

Prior to the finals in South Africa, it was announced that Laurent Blanc would replace Raymond Domenech as French manager. This change might have been expected to deflect a significant amount of criticism of Domenech in his last games in charge. After all, he was already on the way out. But the events surrounding the French participation at the finals were so controversial that Domenech found himself very much in the spotlight once again. Indeed, events off the field proved more disreputable than France's miserable on-field performances.

To begin with, there were reports of dissent within the French camp when Florent Malouda was left on the bench for the first game against Uruguay. Apparently, he objected to playing a defensive midfield role. He was restored to the line-up for the next game after stating his acceptance of his coach's decisions, but then Yoann

Gourcuff was very disappointed to be dropped for the game against Mexico. Following the defeat by Mexico, Domenech would offer no profound analysis of what had gone wrong, but expressed his "disappointment".

Domenech was to reserve one of his most unsporting moments as French coach for virtually his last act in this position, when he refused to shake opposing manager Carlos Alberto Parreira's offered hand at the conclusion of the France–South Africa game. This petty gesture was perhaps a fitting end to his tenure.

> *When the student is ready, the teacher appears.*
> Asian proverb

—10—

The officials – one hundred percent

WHEN WILLIAM GALLAS directed Thierry Henry's cross over the Irish line and into the net, Swedish referee Martin Hansson signalled a goal with an air of confidence, even certainty. Despite the immediate and vociferous protests of goalkeeper Shay Given and several other Irish players that Henry had handled the ball, Hansson had no doubts. Arsenal's manager Arsène Wenger, a Frenchman, boldly stated in a BBC interview after the game that Hansson knew something was wrong with the decision on the basis of the reaction of the Irish players alone. "In the end he gave a goal knowing that it wasn't a goal," said Wenger. The spontaneous reactions of players on the field are often a good indication of what has actually happened, particularly when so many players persist as the Irish did. Yet Irish defender Kevin Kilbane reported Hansson telling him a few minutes later, during the break between the two halves of extra time, that "I can 100% say it wasn't handball." His exact words, said Kilbane.

Under current FIFA regulations, a referee can be 100% certain, and completely wrong. In the aftermath to the game, FIFA upheld the principle that a referee has a right to be wrong. This is all in accordance with the rules. The referee's decision is final, even when it is incorrect. A FIFA source was quoted by the Press Association as saying, "Law 5 states that a referee's decisions on points of fact are final." As discussed in Chapter 8, FIFA has its own unique definition of the word "fact".

Let us look closely at the role that Hansson and his team of officials played in France's qualification for South Africa. To begin, we consider what can be called "the conspiracy theory". According to this theory, the officials deliberately conspired to ensure that France overcame Ireland to reach the finals. We do not believe this to be true. As it happens, paradoxically, the main support for this theory comes from the actions of FIFA, football's governing body.

The late decision by FIFA to seed the teams in the play-offs sent a clear message that they preferred the higher-ranked teams to make it through to the finals. That is, after all, the purpose of seeding. It becomes unfair when seeded teams do not perform according to their seeding, and instead of having to accept the consequences of their underperformance, they are rewarded by being seeded again. The French were the beneficiaries of exactly such a sequence of events. This system gives a decidedly unfair advantage to higher-ranked teams, and makes it ever harder for lower-ranked teams to advance in competitions. Failure to advance results in reduced opportunities to improve, and the seeding system becomes a self-fulfilling process unfair to lower-ranked teams. France qualified for the World Cup finals without having played against any team ranked higher than 20th in the world (Serbia, which finished ahead of France in their qualifying group, were ranked 20th in October 2009), while Ireland was eliminated having had to play four games against teams in the top ten (Italy ranked 4th and France ranked

9th), and after finishing ahead of Bulgaria (ranked 23rd) in their group. Seeding succeeds!

But it needs to be said that even if the play-offs were not seeded, Ireland and France might still have been paired together. Additionally, under FIFA's current outdated rules, Ireland might well have suffered the same cruel fate against any other of the play-off teams had the pairings been different. That being said, there is more to the seeding issue than just the pairings.

The other aspect of FIFA's seeding decision that needs to be considered is the pressure, subtle or not so subtle, that it places on officials in charge of important fixtures. These officials are clearly aware of which teams FIFA prefers at the finals. They are at the same time dependent upon FIFA to choose them to officiate at future important tournaments and matches. The scene is set. Nothing needs to be directly said. The potential for all kinds of pressures on officiating individuals is clear, but may not even be recognised by referees themselves. This pressure is increased by other factors. In the Paris game, minutes before Gallas' goal, the French had claims for a penalty ignored, and had the ball in the Irish net only to be called back (correctly) for offside. Interestingly, all three of Martin Hansson's best-known controversial decisions (Liverpool v. Atletico Madrid, France v. Ireland, and Porto v. Arsenal in the Champions League in 2010) favoured the home team.

To be fair, Martin Hansson's overall performance in the France–Ireland game was reasonably good (shades of ... "Apart from that, Mrs Lincoln, how did you enjoy the play?"). His refereeing decisions did not generally give the appearance of bias. He did not award a penalty against Ireland when he might have done so after Anelka went down in the penalty area. For Gallas' goal, we are prepared to give him the benefit of the doubt and believe his view was obstructed and he did not see Henry handling the ball. The penalty area at the time was crowded with players. Perhaps he could be criticised for not being better positioned. However, without the benefit of video replay, what were his options if he did not see the handball but suspected something was amiss? It appears he received no help from his assistants. The assistant on the line across from the Irish goal did not signal an infringement. Having missed the fact that two French players were offside in the penalty area when the free kick was taken, this assistant apparently also missed the handball. He appeared to have been well enough positioned to see it – in all likelihood he was the best positioned of all four officials, but Hansson got no help from him. Neither did he get any help from the fourth official, far away near the half-way line.

As the whole world watched repeated footage of Henry's double handball, Hansson was left isolated and helpless. But if he did not see it, what was he to do? Giovanni Trapattoni suggested afterwards that he might have asked Henry if he had handled the ball. But Henry might have said, "Yes I did, but not deliberately." What then? In fact, Liam Brady reports Henry saying to him after the game, "I handled it but I didn't mean it."

While the responsibility to make the decision on the field of play falls to the referee, the real fault in a wrong decision like this, we believe, lies elsewhere. Primarily, it lies in Thierry Henry's handling of the ball in the first place (and, as we shall later argue, more importantly in the *second* place). Additionally, FIFA needs to provide referees with appropriate means to help them make correct decisions, not simply support them when they make wrong ones.

Hansson's fellow countrymen were less kind than these authors are in assessing his performance that night. The Swedish newspaper *Aftonbladet* sympathised with what it estimated to be an 80 million strong Irish diaspora, after what it referred to as the "worst mistake by a Swedish referee in over 20 years". The paper suggested that it would be "an insult to the Irish nation" if he were selected to officiate at the World Cup finals in South Africa. They hoped that Hansson and his assistants Stefan Wittberg and Fredrik Nilsson were feeling even worse than the Irish fans were. The Italian *La Gazzetta dello Sport* was just as scathing in its criticism, awarding Hansson a performance score of three out of ten, and calling him "another Moreno". Journalists were also quick to point out that Hansson had been a subject of some controversy previously. Liverpool had benefited from a dubious penalty awarded to them by Hansson in injury time in a Champions League match against Atletico Madrid in 2008. This cost Atletico a place in the last sixteen, and Hansson reported receiving death threats after the game. To be fair, video evidence shows that Hansson's assistant on the line, who was in a better position to see the incident, erroneously called the foul. But what experienced referee will not have made some controversial decision during his career? In fact, if this was the only previous major dubious call he had made in the past, he would appear to have been performing at a higher standard than many of his colleagues. Reports that he had a reputation for questionable calls in the Swedish league were difficult to confirm or refute, but we did note that few of his compatriots appear to have gone on record to defend his reputation after the Paris game. Peter Mikkelsen, a Dane who sits on FIFA's referee selection committee, defended Hansson's refereeing standards based on many games over the years and said that he rarely makes mistakes.

In any comparably contentious issue in other areas of our lives, we have the opportunity to gain greater insight and understanding by getting all sides of the story. In this way, we attempt to arrive at something at least approximating to the truth. So let's hear Martin Hansson's version of what happened and how he saw it.

This would indeed be nice, but unfortunately Hansson had little or nothing to say after the game, apart from a dull "life must go on" comment to a Swedish radio station. The fourth official, Martin Ingvarsson, confirmed upon returning to Sweden that FIFA had forbidden the officials to talk about the match. Hansson is obliged to file a report on the match to FIFA. Unfortunately, these reports are not made public. We do not even know if Hansson is allowed to, or even supposed to, review video evidence from the match before filing his report. Hugh Dallas was the referee's observer at the game and also had to submit a report. Another secret file. It seems that FIFA's policy of keeping reports confidential is at odds with modern values of transparency and accountability. If the intention of such policies is to protect officials from criticism, it is clearly ineffective. Scrutiny and critical appraisal will happen anyway. It will just be less informed.

In the absence of Hansson explaining what happened himself, our story remains incomplete. Trapattoni questioned how referees are chosen for such big games, and why a "Hansson nobody" was put in charge of the game. We do know that he is an experienced referee, and he took charge of the 2009 Confederations Cup final between Brazil and the USA in South Africa. He has been refereeing since he was fifteen years old. Now 38, he obtained his FIFA badge while still in his late twenties. He works as a fireman.

This does not help us much, does it? But one thing does stand out from these basic facts. He is a fireman. It is not important that he is a fireman – he could be a teacher, a farmer, or a traffic cop. But in the world of international football, where transfer fees are measured in tens of millions of euros; where the big club teams have turnovers measured in billions; and where a country's economic performance may be influenced by whether it qualifies for the World Cup finals or not – why are games of such enormous importance officiated by a team of part-timers? We need a cohort of top-class fully professional referees, who will likely be both technically better and less susceptible to outside influences and pressures as a result of that professionalism. And we need to support them with appropriate technology to help them do the best possible job.

More information did emerge later. *The Times* posted an article and analysed still pictures from the incident which suggested that the assistant on the far touchline, Fredrik Nilsson, could have had his view of Henry obscured by the position of Irish goalkeeper Shay Given. However, review of this evidence is inconclusive, as video frame analysis also suggests he might have been in a position to see the handball. He should have seen the two players offside. Nevertheless, his failure to spot the offences was human error, not conspiracy.

Martin Hansson cited *The Times'* analysis as exonerating his decision (and that of his assistants) in the Swedish newspaper *Sydöstran*. Breaking his silence six days after the game, he said, "I realise that it was not my fault. It was an unfortunate event that had big consequences for Ireland, but it wasn't the fault of the refereeing team." Much later, at the World Cup finals in 2010, Hansson admitted shedding a tear when he realised his error in allowing the goal.

It must be emphasised that Martin Hansson is not the first referee to make a decisive poor call in a key World Cup match. Many critical games have been influenced by decisions shown to be completely wrong. The most famous and directly comparable incident is of course the first goal that Diego Maradona scored against England in the quarter-final of the 1986 World Cup. Jumping high together with England goalkeeper Peter Shilton, Maradona directed the ball into the net with his hand – claiming cheekily afterwards that it was partly "the hand of God" that did it. The Tunisian referee failed to see the handball and the goal was given. Argentina won the game 2–1, and went on to win the World Cup. This incident alone should have prompted FIFA to introduce video technology.

In the 2009 Confederations Cup, Brazil and Egypt were tied 3–3 as the game headed into additional time. A Brazilian shot was deflected wide and English referee Howard Webb awarded a corner. He then changed his mind, issued a red card to the Egyptian defender Ahmed al-Muhamadi for handball, and awarded a penalty to Brazil. Kaká scored, and Brazil won 4–3. It was alleged that the fourth official had seen the handball on a video monitor, and informed the referee of the offence. *The Times* reported that FIFA President Blatter responded by banishing all TV screens from tunnels and technical areas.

Interestingly, although FIFA clearly objects to the use of video replay by referees, there does not appear to be a specific rule forbidding this in the Laws of the Game. Graham Poll is a retired Premier League and World Cup referee. In his 2009 book on controversial refereeing decisions, he analysed in detail the Zinedine Zidane head-butting incident in the 2006 World Cup final. Despite denials by FIFA, he concluded that the evidence suggests that the fourth official did make use of video replay in advising the referee about the incident.

So if Martin Hansson did not see Henry handling the ball, and his assistants did not bring it to his attention, there was seemingly little he could do except award a goal. But he can be criticised for poor positioning, and his assistant can be criticised for missing the offsides and the handballs when he might have seen them. Thierry Henry broke the rules and went unpunished. Could Martin Hansson have been strong enough to break the guidelines (not the rules) and come to the sideline and insist on viewing video footage to help him make the right decision? What a hero he would have been then.

Subsequently, Martin Hansson and his team were selected to go to South Africa to officiate at the World Cup finals. However, Fredrik Nilsson was no longer part of the team, and was replaced by Henrik Andren. The selection of Hansson to officiate at the finals was inappropriate. While he may be able to defend his failure to correctly make that crucial call, he must still accept responsibility for that error. To be rewarded with a spot at the finals suggests that it did not matter that he got it so wrong. It also suggests to future referees that it does no harm to help FIFA's preferred teams qualify. In the end, Hansson was not assigned to referee any games at the finals, though he did act as fourth official. Nevertheless, controversial refereeing decisions were still prominent.

One can present people with opportunities.
One cannot make them equal to them.
Rosamond Lehmann

—11—

Video replay – the time has come

THOSE WHO SUPPORT the introduction of video replay technology to the game of football – among whom we include ourselves – hope that it is only a matter of time before this technology will be introduced. Such reforms to the rules of football would make the game more transparent, and more honest. It is hardly a surprise that the great majority of people with a significant direct involvement in the professional game support its introduction.

Arsène Wenger is one of the world's most respected managers. He played a pivotal role in Thierry Henry's rise to stardom, coaching him in his early years at Monaco, and later during his long career at Arsenal. Wenger has repeatedly called for the use of video replay technology. In response to many of the controversial refereeing decisions at the 2002 World Cup, in particular the games that Korea played against Italy and Spain, Wenger said, "It's useless just changing the referees – we have to think how we can help them." He repeated his call in 2006 after Henry, playing for Arsenal, had a goal wrongly disallowed in the Champions League. After Henry's handball against Ireland, in a BBC interview, he pointed out how ridiculous it really is. "We are sitting here in 2009 where two billion people see what happened, and one guy doesn't, and you cannot help him." Sir Alex Ferguson of Manchester United and the English Premier League's most successful manager, is in full agreement. His frustration is evident when he remarks that the overwhelming support for such a move among managers and players around the world means little until FIFA is convinced. Managers Mick McCarthy, Steve Bruce and Pep Guardiola all went on record after the game supporting calls for the introduction of video replay technology. After several controversies at the World Cup finals in 2010, Guss Hiddink called on Sepp Blatter to introduce video replay technology or immediately resign.

Only a few managers do not support the use of video replays. One of these is Phil Brown, who guided Hull City to the English Premier League for the first time in their history in 2008. Interviewed after the Henry handball, he gave his view that video technology should not be part of the game, but did agree with split-second goal-line technology. Nevertheless, he confirmed his opinion that the World Cup final should be played under the same circumstances as a Sunday league game. According to this scenario, had William Gallas re-directed the ball on to the underside of the bar and down on to the goal-line, it would have been correct to use technology to decide if it had crossed the line, but also appropriate to ignore the handball that led to the goal. In addition, all Sunday league game venues would be equipped with split-second goal-line technology!

FIFPro, the international players' union, supports the introduction of technology to assist referees. Tijs Tummers, secretary of FIFPro's technical committee, called the failure to do so "unacceptable", going on to say, "Technology does not undermine the authority of referees, it only helps them."

One group which has been strangely quiet on the issue of video replay technology has been the referees themselves. The most likely reason for this is that referees have no international professional organisation. They are dependent on FIFA and UEFA for their appointments. If FIFA opposes video replay, how can referees speak out on the issue without risking their careers? The furthest any current top-level referee has gone on this issue was the comment by Howard Webb in South Africa in June 2010, when he said, "I'm open-minded about anything that makes us more credible as match officials."

Why exactly does FIFA object to the use of video replay to help referees make the right call at crucial points in a game? It is said that they believe this would "dehumanise" football, and that occasional errors are an integral part of the game. Instead, they have tried to reduce cheating by introducing harsher penalties in certain circumstances – for example, an automatic red card for a foul committed by the last defender against a forward likely to score. They have also encouraged referees to give yellow cards to players who simulate a foul by diving. Unfortunately, this has sometimes resulted in a player being denied a legitimate penalty and then having insult added to injury by finding himself yellow-carded for diving despite being the victim of a foul.

The argument that top-class games should be played under the same rules and circumstances as weekend amateur games does not stand up to scrutiny. Amateur games are often played on poor pitches, with inexperienced referees, and with or without two assistant referees. Most obviously, the rewards at stake in a local league match as opposed to a World Cup match cannot be realistically compared.

FIFA does in fact use technology to a significant degree. Indeed, the organisation would not be what it is today were it not for televised football and all that it brings to the sport. Firstly, it has helped to popularise the sport. Secondly, it has generated an enormous amount of money for the game by selling broadcasting rights for games and tournaments. Broadcasters in turn reap large profits from advertising revenues, made possible by the worldwide popularity of the game.

In fact, FIFA boasts that it uses technology in training referees. "The latest technology has been implemented in the preparation of the referees both within practical training, and interactive sessions, whilst performances at respective FIFA competitions were also analysed and evaluated" (FIFA, 5th February 2010).

Even at the level of the actual game itself, FIFA already embraces technology. Referees and their assistants communicate with each other using audio technology. In an area of even more relevance to the current debate, video footage of games is often used to examine incidents missed by the referee that might result in disciplinary proceedings. However, the criteria for choosing which incidents to review appear to be somewhat haphazard.

In the 2006 World Cup finals, German midfielder Torsten Frings was suspended for the semi-final against Italy. FIFA made this decision after reviewing video footage of the quarter-final match between Germany and Argentina. In a fracas that followed Germany's penalty shoot-out victory, Frings was recorded throwing a punch at Julio Ricardo Cruz. Interestingly, FIFA had originally indicated that no action would be taken, but reportedly changed its mind when video replays of the incident were shown on German and Italian television.

Michel Platini, President of UEFA, has expressed the opinion that video evidence would "destroy football". Despite this opinion, UEFA has published very specific guidelines for television camera positions (fixed and mobile) to record games at the qualifiers for the 2012

European Championship qualifiers. We presume this is to provide reliable footage to review after games are completed. So it is not video evidence which would destroy football, but rather how it is used. It is our contention that the continued refusal to use video replay technology for crucial decisions during the game is more likely to damage the already tarnished reputation of the game.

Officials continue to have great difficulty reliably detecting players who are offside. At the time of the French free kick which led to the goal in Paris against Ireland, William Gallas and Sébastien Squillaci were offside. Both of these players were significantly involved in the subsequent play. Squillaci jumped with Dunne for the incoming ball, arm raised, but both players missed it. Gallas eventually put the ball in the net. In the English Premier League, goals are regularly scored by players who are offside. On 9th February 2010, Fulham defeated Burnley 3–0 in a fixture of importance to both teams in their battle to remain in the Premier League. Both of Fulham's first two goals should have been disallowed for offside infringements. Wigan manager Roberto Martinez claimed the Premier League is being made to look a laughing stock by poor refereeing decisions. After Tottenham Hotspurs' opening goal against his side on 21st February 2010 was allowed despite the scorer being clearly offside, Martinez noted that it was "not even a close call". These are just recent examples. Many more could be cited.

The same thing happens regularly in the prestigious Champions League. In the first round of the 2009–2010 knock-out phase, Bayern Munich defeated Fiorentina 2–1 in Munich. The scorer of the winning goal was offside. On this occasion, referee Tom Henning Ovrebro afterwards admitted he should have disallowed Miroslav Klose's late winner. The goal proved decisive in the tie, as Bayern advanced to the quarter-finals on the away goals rule after Fiorentina won the second leg 3–2.

In the round of sixteen at the World Cup finals in 2010, Argentina's opening goal against Mexico was allowed despite the fact that goalscorer Carlos Tevez was clearly offside at the time the ball was passed to him. Contrary to FIFA policy, the incident was replayed on the giant screens at the game. The Mexicans protested to no avail. Italian referee Roberto Rosetti, who had also been involved in the controversial sending off of Australia's Harry Kewell against Ghana, was given no further assignments at the World Cup. He retired after the tournament. Mexico received an apology from Sepp Blatter, and FIFA promised to ensure that spectators were not shown controversial replays during games. But the illegal goal stood, and helped Argentina towards a 3–1 victory, and a place in the quarter-finals.

While video replay technology is not absolutely reliable, it would certainly be a big improvement on the current situation. In fact, the accurate detection of offside could be considered the ideal circumstance for video replay to demonstrate its advantages over human decision making. Many more correct calls would be made. Furthermore, there would be one less opportunity for officials to potentially bias their decisions in favour of one team.

Of all the major sports, football is the lowest-scoring one. At the highest levels, 0–0 draws are not at all unusual, and important games are often decided by a single goal. Indeed, two of the last five World Cup finals have been decided on penalty kicks after tied games. By comparison, basketball scores are often in the high 90's or 100's, rugby and American football (NFL) teams often score 20 or more points, and ice hockey and baseball too are much higher scoring games than football. Because football match results frequently hinge on a small number of incidents (often one alone), it is crucial to the legitimacy of the game to ensure that correct decisions are made by referees. George Vecsey, writing in *The New York Times* after Frank Lampard's disallowed goal at the World Cup finals in 2010, described football goals as "too precious to be squandered".

Nearly every other major sport now uses video technology during the game to help officials make the best decisions. In ice hockey, video is used only to adjudicate whether the puck has crossed the line, in baseball to determine whether the ball has left the playing area in a home run call, and in rugby, a television match official can be called upon to help decide if a try has been scored. Basketball uses video replay to determine timing reviews, discipline issues, and to decide if a shot was from two- or three-point range. A tennis player can challenge a ruling three times in each set, but does not use up a challenge if he proves to be correct. In the NFL, the officials themselves may decide upon a video review, and each head coach can challenge a ruling twice per game (and a third time also if both previous challenges were correct) by throwing a flag. If a video review fails to show evidence to change the original call, or is indeterminate, the original ruling stands. As a result of such transparency, NFL referees are a highly respected group, and are widely viewed as officials doing their very best to make fair and correct decisions. Many North Americans have difficulty understanding football's reluctance to avail of this relatively simple way of ensuring fair play. Canadian Adam Gopnik, writing in the *New Yorker* on how to get a penalty in football, suggested "walk into the 'area' with the ball, get breathed on hard, and then immediately collapse".

The exact circumstances under which video replay should be used in football are not completely clear, and would probably evolve somewhat as experience is gained. Initially, it could be restricted to incidents surrounding the scoring or disallowing of a goal. Some might argue that it should also be used in relation to all red card offences, and all major incidents in the last five minutes of play. The call for a video review might be made by the referee or one of the other three officials, and team managers might also have the right to demand video review on a number of occasions during the game. Certainly, we do not advocate using video replay to help decide on simple fouls or on whose throw-in it is.

Therefore, our specific recommendation is that video replay technology should be initially introduced to assist referees with determining the legitimacy or otherwise of a goal. A video referee should communicate his decision to the on-field official through his earpiece (similar to the system used in rugby union). In exceptional circumstances, either of these two officials could also call for a review of video evidence of other events, such as violent conduct by a player. Such a system would not cause undue delays to the game, nor would it involve the referee even leaving the pitch. For those who value the human element in the game, the vast majority of decisions in the game would still be judgment calls made by the officials. We do not agree with the proposal to use goal-line technology alone. This could lead to the farcical situation whereby a player directs the ball towards the goal with his hand, it manages to cross the line, and a goal is awarded despite the handball offence.

With years of comparable experience in other sports, it should not be too difficult a task for FIFA to speed up the introduction of appropriate rules and guidelines for the use of video replay. What process is involved in changing the rules to allow referees to avail of video replay?

Strangely enough, FIFA on its own could not decide to introduce video replay to football. That decision, pertaining as it does to the laws of the game, must be made by the International Football

Association Board (IFAB). This group first met in 1886 when the football associations of England, Scotland, Wales and Ireland decided to standardise the laws of the game, which varied in different countries at that time. FIFA and the IFAB agreed in 1946 that the IFAB would be the custodian of the game's laws, and this was formalised in the revised FIFA statutes approved in 2003. Nowadays, the IFAB consists of the four "home" associations (with Northern Ireland replacing Ireland), together with four FIFA representatives. For the laws to be changed, a two-thirds voting majority is necessary. In practice, this means that FIFA (which usually votes as a bloc) and at least two of the other associations must be in favour of a proposal.

The FIFA website attempts to explain why the IFAB is viewed as a conservative organisation and why change comes slowly to the rules of football. It says, "The attraction of the game of football resides in its simplicity. And as guardian to its Laws, the IFAB seeks to preserve the original seeds on which the football [sic] has blossomed so spectacularly." Sepp Blatter has also pointed to the entertainment value of controversy, saying, "Fans love to debate any given incident in a game. It is part of the human nature of our sport." Critics claim that the use of video replay will not alter the game's simplicity, but simply make the game fairer, and ensure that the basic laws of the game are consistently applied.

In March 2010, the IFAB rejected calls for the introduction of video replay technology. As expected, the four FIFA delegates voted together against video replay, and were supported by the Welsh and the Northern Irish delegates. The English and Scottish were in favour. FIFA general secretary Jerome Valcke said, "The door is closed. The decision was not to go ahead with technology at all." Minutes after the decision was announced, Birmingham had a crucial goal wrongly disallowed in an FA Cup tie against Portsmouth.

Officials failed to notice that the ball had crossed the line before being scooped away by the Portsmouth goalkeeper. It is not clear if the four "home country" participants at the IFAB meeting were true representatives, bringing the considered opinion of their associations to the meeting, or if they simply voted according to their personal opinions at the time. From comments made after the meeting it seemed that those against video technology placed more value on the "entertainment" element of controversy in the game, than on ensuring justice and fair play. Patrick Nelson of the (Northern) Irish FA said, "We very much appreciate the human side of the game, the debate, the controversy..." Jonathan Ford, CEO of the Football Association of Wales, said: "The human element of the game is the critical element of it. The debate they had with the goal in the 1966 final – that's still being talked about in pubs and that's the beauty of the game and keeping the game alive." We disagree, because this attitude makes it easier for a culture of rule-bending and cheating to flourish. Is Thierry Henry's handball appreciated for its controversy? Should it be accepted as something beautiful which keeps the game alive? We think not. The IFAB vote against video replay technology was not made based upon a trial evaluation in top-class games. It was a vote against evaluating the technology.

Retired international referee Graham Poll states that it is "madness" not to use video replay technology to assist referees, and that the World Cup itself risks ending in "farce" as a result. Commenting on the IFAB decision, he said it reflected a "level of arrogance" within the game. "Beyond comprehension" was how Arsène Wenger described the decision. We are reminded of one definition of a committee: "A group of people who individually can do nothing, but as a group decide that nothing can be done." FIFA secretary general Jerome Valcke said after the IFAB decision that "Questions will always come, we just hope they will not come in the final of the World Cup." Our view is that rather than "hope", we should take action.

With the margin between winning and losing so small in international football today, players and managers continue to seek ways to gain an advantage over opponents. Unfortunately, as things stand, one of the most effective ways is to cheat. This can be done by manufacturing a foul for a free kick or penalty, deceiving a referee into red-carding an opponent, or by a more blatant offense such as scoring a goal with help from a handball. The most effective and reliable way to eliminate such things is by allowing video replay. Cheating offences would become less common as the likelihood of being detected increases. At the same time, referees would be able to avoid making basic errors of judgment such as those related to whether a ball crossed the goal-line or not. Evidently, this would improve the game. Teams would be forced to seek legitimate ways to improve their chances of winning. It would stimulate the advancement of skills (both physical and mental), and innovative developments in preparation, tactics and strategies.

The 2010 World Cup finals in South Africa will be remembered for several reasons. Spain deservedly won the World Cup for the first time, the French were eliminated in embarrassing circumstances, and calls for the introduction of video replay technology became even louder after a series of poor refereeing decisions. The response from FIFA was to apologise to the teams of England and Mexico (the victims of two of the most crucial and blatant missed calls), to change the referees, and to "tighten up" on their policy of not allowing "controversial action" to be shown on the giant screens at game venues. There have been new vague promises from FIFA to re-examine the possible use of technology to assist referees in the future. What action will be taken remains to be seen. After November 2009, Sepp Blatter had stated: "We have six months to show to the world that we have changed because of what has happened in the last [qualifying] matches of the World Cup. If we are not able to do so, we will put our papers under the desk and go home. We must do it." You know what happened.

It is perfectly possible for the laws of the game to be amended to allow the appropriate use of video replay to help referees make crucial decisions. This would mean that proper rules and guidelines could be in place in time for the qualifiers and finals of the World Cup in Brazil in 2014. We earnestly hope that this comes to pass.

Errare humanum est, sed perseverare diabolicum.
Seneca

—12—

FIFA – keeping football in the past

THE FIFA FAIR Play Code for football is crystal clear: "Winning is without value if victory has been achieved unfairly or dishonestly. Cheating is easy but brings no pleasure. Playing fair requires courage and character... and games are pointless unless played fairly." What use are words without action? In world football, the culture of winning at all costs has been allowed to develop without serious and effective attempts to curtail it. The governing body of football has allowed the beautiful game to descend to a state of near farce. Regularly, games at the highest level are decided by illegitimate means. Players fake fouls and injuries. Forwards dive for penalties. Officials miss offside goals. Scoring is assisted by beach balls and handballs.

It has reached the point where some followers of the game are becoming increasingly suspicious that FIFA is deliberately refusing to use modern means of improving the standard of officiating because it would seriously interfere with the ability to influence game results. Such suspicions increase when FIFA is seen to openly favour certain teams above others.

Following the France–Ireland encounter on 18th November 2009, the match reports on the FIFA and UEFA websites both failed to mention Henry's handball. The reports were described as "laughable", but football fans were angry, not amused. To pretend that the highest profile moment in global football since Zinedine Zidane's head-butt in the 2006 World Cup final simply did not happen must be the ultimate act of "mental reservation". Evan Fanning, writing in the *Sunday Independent*, commented that "Even *Pravda* would be embarrassed by that level of propaganda."

The FIFA match report appeared to describe a fictional goal. "France skipper Thierry Henry won the match for the hosts when his angled pass amid a goalmouth scramble was met by the head of William Gallas." France did not win the match. It ended 1–1. None of the millions who watched witnessed a goalmouth scramble. Gallas said afterwards it went in off his shoulder. The UEFA report was no better. "And so came extra-time where in the eighth minute a hopeful France free-kick found its way to Henry, who squared for Gallas to head the goal that takes his country to South Africa." The major difference seems to be that the "angle" has become a "square". The incident came thirteen minutes into extra time, not eight. Neither report mentioned Henry's double handball. Neither report mentioned the fact that two French players were offside when the free kick was taken, one of whom was goal-scorer Gallas. The "fact" that Thierry Henry handled the ball twice had been erased from the record of events, supplanted by the final and un-appealable "truth" of an erroneous referee's decision.

After the outcry around the world about the incident, FIFA revised its online match report. In the new version, they wrote: "William Gallas bundled the ball home to win the match for *Les Bleus* after being set up by Thierry Henry, who later admitted that he had handled in the build-up." The report ends: "France's late stroke of luck finally proved the visitors' downfall." There was no note that the original report had been removed and revised.

Controversy is not new to World Cup football. England won the World Cup in 1966 despite the fact, now generally agreed, that their decisive third goal never crossed the line. Maradona's handball goal helped Argentina progress past England on their way to World Cup victory in 1986. Yet today, 44 years after Geoff Hurst's volley rebounded downwards off the underside of the bar, we still depend on the human eye to make crucial decisions about fleeting moments.

In the round of sixteen at the World Cup finals in South Africa, Germany was leading England 2–1 approaching half-time. A Frank Lampard shot from the edge of the penalty area hit the underside of the bar and bounced down well past the goal line, before the spin of the ball brought it back into the hands of the German goalkeeper, Manuel Neuer. Uruguayan referee Jorge Larrionda did not award a goal, and Germany went on to win 4–1 with two counter-attacking goals in the second half. While many argued that the Germans were the superior team and would have won regardless, the failure to award a goal at the time was a crucial missed call which changed the complexion of the game. Neuer tried to take some "credit" for the officials' error, saying afterwards, "I realised it was over the line and I think the way I carried on so quickly fooled the referee into thinking it was not over."

FIFA (Fédération Internationale de Football Association) was founded in Paris in 1904, and has 208 member associations (sixteen more than the United Nations). It assumed responsibility for organising and governing international football and in particular, since 1930, the World Cup. FIFA provides four out of the eight delegates on the International Football Association Board (IFAB), which is responsible for the laws of football. A FIFA Congress is held once a year, and is made up of representatives of each member association. Changes to FIFA's statutes must be approved by Congress. FIFA's executive committee, chaired by the president, meanwhile makes the day-to-day decisions.

Joseph 'Sepp' Blatter is the Swiss-born president of FIFA. Prior to his election as president in 1998, he served as technical director (1975–1981), and general secretary (1981–1998). He is currently serving his third term in office as president. He is also a member of the International Olympic Committee (IOC), and is on the board of the World Anti-Doping Agency (WADA). In the foreword to the 1998 book *Ultimate Soccer* (by Ivor Baddiel), Blatter says, "The game loses much of its enjoyment if we don't remember the rules of Fair Play," and continues, "The great players didn't need to foul or cheat to prove how good they were."

The first controversy regarding the Ireland-France play-off resulted from the decision by FIFA's executive committee on 29th September to seed the teams for the play-off draw. This prevented the higher-ranked teams from being paired against each other. At the time that the decision was made, it was likely that France, Portugal and either Germany or Russia would be in the play-offs. The executive committee has members from Russia, Germany and France, and its general secretary is French. None of the four lowest-ranked play-off qualifiers have a representative on FIFA's executive. Many observers criticised this late decision for two reasons. Firstly, it amounted in fact to an alteration in the rules of an event while that event was in progress. Secondly, it was seen as giving an unfair advantage to certain teams, and was perceived as sending a message to all involved as to which teams FIFA preferred to have as participants in the finals. After this criticism, Sepp Blatter admitted in October

2009 that the issue had been badly handled. "It should have been announced earlier," he said, indicating that changes would be made for the 2014 event. If the recently published regulations for UEFA's European Championships 2012 are anything to go by (second-placed teams will be seeded for the play-off draw), then the changes he speaks of are likely to simply mean announcing from the beginning that play-off draws will be seeded. This fails to address the second criticism. As Giovanni Trapattoni said, "Every country has the right to qualify. This draw must be open to give the same opportunity to everybody."

In qualifying for the World Cup finals, France enjoyed the benefit of being seeded twice. As a result, they qualified for the finals without having to play against any team ranked higher than Serbia, the winners of France's qualification group. Serbia was 20th on the FIFA ranking list in October 2009. Ireland, on the other hand, would not be at the finals despite losing only one of twelve games, four of which were against teams from the world's top ten (Italy ranked 4th, and France ranked 9th, both twice), and finishing above Bulgaria (ranked 23rd) in their group. Ireland had to battle against the current world champions and current vice-champions in their efforts to reach the finals.

In retrospect, Blatter's further comments in October 2009 on the issue of World Cup qualification seem surreal. "All the best teams are there. If someone has missed out it is because they haven't deserved it." With FIFA having done so much to help the higher-ranked teams to qualify, it is not clear if he was thinking of France, or of Ireland.

However, immediately after France's undeserved qualification, Blatter was atypically quiet. Despite calls for him to issue a statement, and direct criticism aimed at him by Irish captain Robbie Keane and manager Giovanni Trapattoni, no immediate response was forthcoming. "I would like to know what I have done to Blatter," Trapattoni said. "If he explains it to me at least I would be calm."

On 23rd November, FIFA announced that there would be an extraordinary meeting of the executive council on 2nd December 2009 to discuss, among other things, "incidents at the play-offs". Two days prior to this meeting, Blatter spoke publically for the first time about the issue. He reiterated the impossibility of the game being replayed, and ridiculed an FAI suggestion that Ireland be included as an extra team at the World Cup finals ("They have asked for that, really," he told the assembled media). He did agree that something had to be done about helping referees make better decisions. He mentioned the possibility of extra officials, but not of video replay. He called Henry's action "a cheating handball".

Liam Brady was quick to call Blatter an "embarrassment" and a "loose cannon" for making a public mockery of a privately discussed proposal which the FAI never expected to be taken seriously. Blatter apologised, or did he? Rather, as Emmet Malone writing in *The Irish Times* pointed out, he "provided a wonderfully qualified expression of regret for everybody else's behaviour in relation to his handling of the matter". Blatter said, "I would like to express my regrets to a wrong interpretation of what I said..."

Later Blatter suggested that Ireland might receive some sort of "moral compensation" for the manner of their elimination. Richard Dunne was unimpressed. "What's this award that FIFA are going to give to Ireland? It is FIFA taking the mickey – give the Irish a plaque instead of going to the World Cup." The FAI released a statement to emphasise instead the real focus of their meeting with FIFA. They proposed (1) a ban on changing rules in mid-tournament, (2) the introduction of video replay technology, and (3) stronger sanctions for players involved in match-defining breaches of the laws.

At the meeting on 2nd December, FIFA's executive committee rejected the possibility of having extra match officials at the World Cup finals in South Africa. No mention was made of video replay technology. Sepp Blatter appealed to all players and coaches to observe fair play. So no real progress has been made, and the possibility remains that a team can cheat its way to becoming World Cup champions.

In January 2010, FIFA announced that there was no basis for taking any action against Thierry Henry for his handball offence against Ireland, which helped France to qualify for the World Cup finals. Henry's representatives successfully argued that his handball was not a "serious infringement". According to Article 77a of FIFA's disciplinary code, using one's hand to prevent a goal being scored is considered a serious offence, but using one's hand to help score a goal is not. Irish defender Seán St Ledger claimed the decision would not dissuade others from cheating in the future, and pointed out that "they said they've got no legal foundation but they still had the power to change the rules and introduce the seedings."

"The challenge for football, and for FIFA specifically, in the wake of the Henry affair, is to properly attack the culture of cheating," wrote Jim Holden in *World Soccer* magazine. While stopping well short of advocating access to video replay for refereeing decisions, Holden makes a strong case for severe sanctions against players shown to have cheated in a game, and speaks of the toothless and ineffective Fair Play campaign. However, this alone does not go nearly far enough, and many teams might be willing to sacrifice a player to suspension if they gained an important victory through his cheating offence. We need more severe sanctions *and* access to video replay technology for referees. Serious consideration should also be given to sanctioning teams as well as individuals for cheating offences. Then we could expect to see some real progress. To echo the spirit of FIFA's own Fair Play code, cheating should not only be condemned as unacceptable, it should be legislated as unacceptable. It must be punishable by severe sanctions, possibly even disqualification.

It is a sad to realise that today, the issue as to whether or not there is a culture of cheating in top level sport is hardly considered worth debating. From the fixing of Baseball's World Series in 1919, to Renault's Formula One team instructing a driver to crash at the Singapore Grand Prix in 2008, there are scores of examples. What is worth considering here is whether in international football FIFA has done enough to eliminate this culture, taken a neutral stance, or by failing to take effective action, has allowed such a culture to flourish?

What were the consequences of Diego Maradona's handball against England in the 1986 World Cup? The most obvious one was that the goal was allowed to stand and helped Argentina progress in the competition, which they eventually won. Maradona received no sanction from FIFA, although the incident remained a large and permanent stain on his reputation (more stains appeared later). Nevertheless, this cheating goal stood, and the world saw that breaking the rules succeeded.

Fast-forward to the World Cup of 2002 in Japan and Korea. Here we saw another example of successful cheating. Turkish defender Hakan Ünsal kicked the ball towards Brazil's Rivaldo at the corner flag. The ball struck his thigh, but Rivaldo fell to the ground clutching his face. The Turkish player was sent off with a second yellow card. After a video review, Rivaldo was fined 10,000 Swiss Francs by FIFA. It was pointed out that this was less than half a day's pay for him. He refused to express regret for the incident, saying play-acting was part of the game. Rivaldo was FIFA's World Player of the Year in 1999. Referees seem particularly prone to react sympathetically to a player who falls down with his hands over his face – Thiago Motta of Inter Milan (in the Champions League semi-final against Barcelona), and Kaka of Brazil (at the World Cup against Côte d'Ivoire) both received controversial red cards as a result of such "play-acting" by opponents.

At the 2002 finals, the controversies surrounding the surprising progress of the South Korean team to the semi-finals were more serious. Italy was eliminated in the round of 16 by South Korea after several controversial refereeing decisions by Ecuadorian referee Byron Moreno. Italians suspected a conspiracy to ensure the Koreans stayed in the competition. FIFA denied this and Sepp Blatter pointed to other game events which contributed to Italy's loss. However, in September of the same year, FIFA announced that they were launching an investigation "as a result of a number of controversies regarding referee Byron Moreno in Japan, Italy, and South America over the past few months". Moreno was then banned in Ecuador for 20 matches after a game in which he added 12 minutes of injury time during which the home team scored twice to win 4–3. On his return from that ban, he was then almost immediately banned again after sending off three players from the same team. Moreno retired from refereeing in June 2003, claiming he was "leaving through the front door with my head held high". The Spanish football press dismissed Italian complaints about their World Cup defeat, but they were soon to change their minds.

Gamal Mahmoud Ahmed Al-Ghandour was the Egyptian referee of South Korea's next match, their quarter-final against Spain. The Spaniards had two legitimate goals disallowed, and eventually lost on penalties. Paul Hayward, writing in *The Telegraph*, said South Korea had no right to be in the semi-finals, and that the "tournament has descended into farce". Spain's Ivan Helguera said, "Everyone saw two perfectly good goals. If Spain didn't win, it's because they didn't want us to win." *La Nacion*, the Argentinean paper, wrote: "This World Cup should be declared null and void." To his credit, Sepp Blatter did acknowledge that some of the officiating at the finals was "a disaster". However, a FIFA spokesperson called the conspiracy theories "pathetic". *BBC Sport* reported accusations by a Spanish sports daily that Al-Ghandour had accepted a Hyundai car as a "gift" from FIFA vice-president Chung Mong-Joon, a South Korean. Al-Ghandour threatened to sue for libel, but he seems not to have pursued this threat. However, these simplistic allegations are hardly credible. Nevertheless, the Spain-South Korea game was his last international game, and he retired from refereeing at the end of 2002.

The Japan-Korea World Cup of 2002 was a public relations disaster for FIFA, and a poor advertisement for honesty in the game. It showed that FIFA did not have effective measures in place to ensure fair play. The controversial games were widely analysed because of the involvement of Italy and Spain, two of the countries where football is most popular. It also confirmed to those who wished to gain an advantage by cheating that they could successfully do so. The referee was always right, and decisions and results could not be reversed. FIFA's response to breaches of fair play was to either ignore them, defend them, or to act in a manner that was clearly "too little too late".

The World Cup finals of 2010 featured many controversial moments and poor refereeing decisions. We have discussed some of these elsewhere in this book – Lampard's disallowed goal against Germany, Tevez's offside goal against Mexico, and Fabiano's goal involving a double handball against Côte d'Ivoire. The USA had two seemingly valid goals disallowed in the group stage (against Slovenia and Algeria). To be fair, there were also some excellent refereeing performances at the finals, such as those of Ravshan Irmatov of

Uzbekistan (Argentina–Germany), Yuichi Nishimura of Japan (Netherlands–Brazil), and Viktor Kassai of Hungary (Germany–Spain). FIFA's analysis showed that 96% of referees' decisions were correct at the finals, and compared this to a 60% success rate in players scoring from penalties (9 out of 16).

In the aftermath of the Paris game, Giovanni Trapattoni said that many of the game's ills can be traced to special interests, and ultimately greed and money. We will not get involved in discussing specific amounts, but it is clear that enormous amounts of money are involved in the World Cup. When such amounts are at stake, there will always be those who will try to exploit whatever loopholes they can identify to their advantage.

Additionally, although there are a number of democratic processes in international football governance, several key executives are particularly influential in how things are run and the decisions that are made – people such as Sepp Blatter, Michel Platini, Issa Hayatou and Chung Mong-Joon. They are among the members of the executive committee, and it is this committee which appoints the four FIFA "representatives" to sit on the eight-member IFAB, which is responsible for the game's rules. Mr Hayatou is the president of the Confederation of African Football (CAF), which had recently banned Togo from the next two African Nations Cup competitions. Togo had withdrawn late from the Angolan finals in 2010 after their team bus was assaulted by rebels, killing three members of their entourage. The ban was imposed because the CAF stated that there had been political interference in the decision to withdraw. There were widespread calls for Hayatou's resignation after this decision, which was eventually reversed.

FIFA's efforts at ensuring fair play and justice in football have been at best well-meaning and naive, but at worst ineffective and irresolute. The key to this issue is transparency. FIFA's own mission statement includes the following sentence: "We believe that, just as the game itself, FIFA must be a model of fair play, tolerance, sportsmanship and transparency." Transparency should not include secret referees' reports, should not accept hastily changing the rules of a tournament to the advantage of certain teams, and should not include publishing inaccurate match reports. But above all, transparency should not permit a scenario where a referee can make a crucial decision that the watching world sees clearly to be incorrect. "The camera cannot lie." Alan Ruddock, writing in the *Sunday Independent* the weekend after the Paris game, asked: "Will they introduce technology? Will they punish Henry? Will they send Hansson and the French team to South Africa?" The reader knows the answers.

Those who run world football could do worse than take seriously the proposals made by the FAI to FIFA in the aftermath of the Henry handball. Rules should be consistent and fair to all teams, referees should have access to video replay technology for crucial decisions, and serious sanctions should be enforced where appropriate. These might be directed at an offending official, an offending player, but also in some circumstances at offending teams.

Serious sport has nothing to do with fair play.
George Orwell

—13—

Who is Thierry Henry?

THERE IS NO doubt about it. Thierry Henry is one of football's most talented players and he has had a phenomenally successful career. At the time of his handball, he played with then-reigning European and World Club Champions Barcelona, and in summer 2010 was transferred to New York Red Bulls.

Born on 17th August 1977 in Paris, his career in top flight football began in Monaco under manager Arsène Wenger. In 1996, he signed an agreement to join Real Madrid while still under contract with Monaco. FIFA blocked the transfer and Henry was fined. After a short spell at Juventus, he signed for Wenger's Arsenal in 1999. He is Arsenal's all-time leading scorer, with 226 goals in 369 appearances, and was the English Premier League's top scorer four times within six seasons. During his time at Arsenal (1999–2007) he won the PFA Players' Player of the Year award twice, and the Football Writers' Association Footballer of the Year award three times. He was twice runner-up in the FIFA World Player of the Year award, second to Zinedine Zidane in 2003, and to Ronaldinho in 2004. He was transferred from Arsenal to Barcelona in 2007.

Henry played his first game for France in a friendly against South Africa in 1997, and is the second most capped French player, after Lilian Thuram who has played 142 times for his country. Henry has played 123 times for France. He is also France's all-time top scorer, with a record 51 goals. He was France's top scorer at the World Cup finals in 1998 with three goals, but he did not play in the final match against Brazil. His planned appearance as a substitute in that game did not happen because of the team reorganisation necessary after Marcel Desailly was sent off. Henry was voted man of the match in three games during the European Championship finals in 2000, including the final when France beat Italy 2–1. At the 2002 World Cup finals in Japan, Henry was red carded after 24 minutes against Uruguay. The game ended 0–0 and he was suspended for France's last group game against Denmark. The Danes won 2–0 and France was eliminated. Henry scored three goals at the 2006 World Cup finals in Germany, including the vital winning score against Brazil in the quarter-final. He was replaced by substitute Sylvain Wiltord during extra time in the final against Italy, so he did not participate in the penalty shoot-out. After spending most of the South Africa World Cup on the bench, Henry announced his retirement from international football in July 2010.

Henry has played as a winger and a centre forward. He had a tendency to drift to different positions during a game, losing his marker and creating space for attacking colleagues. In his prime, he was noted for his pace and acceleration. Technically, he was considered excellent apart from a weakness in heading ability. His play has been marked by an intelligence and creativity often lacking in lesser players. Many considered him one of the most effective players in a one-on-one situation. He is remarkably unselfish on the pitch – a true team player, creating many goal opportunities for his team-mates. He was also the regular free-kick and penalty taker when with Arsenal, except when he himself was the player fouled for a penalty. During the 2004 season, he famously scored free-kick goals against Chelsea and Aston Villa while they were still organising their defensive formations. He appeared to have asked the referee on each occasion whether he could proceed to take the kick. These incidents led to a change in the way officials manage such free kicks.

In 2006, playing for Arsenal against CSKA in the Champions League, Henry had a goal disallowed after he was wrongly judged to have handled the ball. Thierry Henry was "fuming" at the decision, pointing out that the goalkeeper and defenders did not call for a handball (!) and stated in a BBC interview: "I just hope that what goes around comes around and it'll be our turn next time." While his manager Wenger used the incident to repeat his calls for video replay technology to be introduced, Henry was wishing for some kind of evening-of-the-score in the future by a similar bad call.

Thierry Henry did have a reputation for fair play. His red card against Uruguay in the 2002 World Cup was justifiable, and costly for his team, but his foul appeared to be more clumsy than intentional. However, in the 2006 World Cup finals, he angered many fans (especially in Spain) when he appeared to fake a facial injury after a challenge from Carles Puyol. Many were reminded of his comments after his Arsenal team had lost the Champions League final to Barcelona a few weeks earlier. Henry complained of how Puyol had played and said, "Maybe next time I'll learn how to dive."

Off the field, Henry has promoted children's welfare through a UNICEF-FIFA initiative, is a leader of the anti-racism campaign *Stand Up Speak Up*, and has helped raise funds for Cystic Fibrosis and AIDS research. He has earned millions of euros by endorsing the products of Nike, Renault, Reebok, Pepsi, Gillette and others. The advertisements he appeared in for the Renault Clio resulted in the word "va-va-voom" being later included in the *Oxford English Dictionary*. In one of these videos, the script has him saying, "Look, I don't make the rules." In late 2009, the fact that the public image of Gillette was represented by Thierry Henry and Tiger Woods (along with Roger Federer) was widely commented upon. Their *Champions Programme* claimed to feature three of the "best-known, most widely respected and successful athletes competing today".

Henry was awarded the title of Chevalier of the Légion d'Honneur in 1998, along with the rest of the French World Cup squad. *Time* magazine in 2007 included Henry as one of the top 100 most influential people in the world, citing not only his football skills, but also his high-profile stand against racism. It takes years to build such a reputation, but it can be tarnished in a matter of seconds. In 2010, *Time* listed Henry's handball in second place on its updated list of *Top Ten Sporting Cheats*.

The facts pertaining to Henry's handball are not in dispute. When the free kick from Florent Malouda floated over the players in the crowded penalty area, the ball arrived to Henry near the goal line a few yards to the left of the goal, behind Irish defender Paul McShane. It struck Henry's left arm, which was extended downwards at his side. This prevented the ball going out of play. Henry then lifted this arm so that the palm of his hand controlled the ball further, and with a raised foot crossed for William Gallas to score from directly in front of the goal. Referee Martin Hansson awarded a goal.

Henry then ran around the back of the Irish goal to join in the French celebrations of the "goal" that would send them to the World Cup finals. The low esteem in which Henry is held by Irish supporters probably has as much to do with these celebrations as the handball itself.

After the final whistle confirmed France's 2–1 aggregate victory over Ireland, Thierry Henry sought out Richard Dunne, and sat quietly beside him on the pitch. Afterwards, the two players exchanged a perfunctory hug. Dunne reported that Henry admitted the handball but that it was something that "just happened" and that he had not "intended it". Dunne himself is a player worthy of admiration. After being transferred from Manchester City to Aston Villa, he scored for Villa in the next encounter between the two teams. Out of respect for his former supporters, he declined to celebrate the goal. Eric Cantona was most appalled by Henry trying to console Dunne, and would have been less forgiving in the circumstances, saying: "If I had been an Irishman, he wouldn't have lasted three seconds." Dunne later admitted that at the time, he did not really appreciate the extent of Henry's involvement in the move that led to the goal. He only saw it on video afterwards in the dressing room. Speaking to RTE, he said, "He sat down with me. He just said he'd handled it but he didn't mean it. I hadn't seen then how blatantly he had handled it."

Afterwards, Henry initially dismissed criticism by stating, "I am not the referee." Of course, it is the referee's responsibility to enforce the rules, but players are expected to adhere to the rules. Imagine the chaos if all players adopted the attitude that they can play as they wish, because the sole responsibility for game conduct falls to the referee. This logic has clear limitations. Henry was quoted in *Le Figaro* as saying, "I am not going to lie," and admitted a handball. He then continued by saying, "the ball hit my hand and I continued to play." The television replays of the incident show that the ball hit Henry's arm, after which he blatantly controlled the ball with his hand.

Thierry Henry cheated, but he is not the first player who has cheated by handling the ball to secure an advantage for his team, nor will he be the last. Diego Maradona did it famously in 1986 against

England. Afterwards, he commented that he had to encourage his team-mates to celebrate the goal with him because they were expecting it to be disallowed. *The Sun* newspaper claimed in an interview published in January 2008 that he issued his first ever apology for the incident. But even a belated apology proved to be no apology at all, because what he actually said was, "If I could apologise and go back and change history I would do. But the goal is still a goal." Lionel Messi also scored with a handball, playing for Barcelona against Espanyol in 2007. Handball goals are not limited to Argentinean superstars – there are many other instances.

Two incidents at the World Cup finals in South Africa deserve mention here. In the group game between Brazil and Côte d'Ivoire, Luis Fabiano handled the ball twice in the run-up to his second goal. The goal was allowed to stand. French referee Stephane Lannoy was seen questioning Fabiano by gesture if he had handled, and Fabiano appeared to indicate that he did not. After the game, he admitted the offence, but showed no remorse. "It seems as though the ball hit my hand and the second time it hit my shoulder, but to make the goal more beautiful there needed to be a bit of doubt."

In the quarter-finals, Uruguay's Luis Suarez prevented a winning goal for Ghana by handling the ball on the line in the last moments of extra time. He was correctly red-carded, and Ghana was awarded a penalty, which was missed. Uruguay went on to win the tie on penalty kicks. While some compared Suarez's actions to those of Henry and criticised him for cheating, there are several key differences. His offence was detected, and his punishment followed the laws of the game, and included his exclusion from Uruguay's semi-final match. Ghana's failure to convert the spot-kick is hardly a reason to justify changing the laws of the game as advocated by some who called for the awarding of a goal in such circumstances (comparing it to the penalty try in Rugby Union). Nevertheless, Suarez's post-game comments that "the hand of God now belongs to me" did not endear him to many true football fans outside of Uruguay.

What mitigating factors can there be for Thierry Henry in the circumstances of his handball? At least in this instance we are allowed to hear what he had to say for himself. Two days after the game, Thierry Henry issued a statement about what happened, reproduced in its entirety below.

> *I have said at the time and I will say again that yes I handled the ball. I am not a cheat and never have been. It was an instinctive reaction to a ball that was coming extremely fast in a crowded penalty area. As a footballer you do not have the luxury of the television to slow the pace of the ball down 100 times to be able to make a conscious decision. People are viewing a slow motion version of what happened and not what I or any other footballer faces in the game. If people look at it in full speed you will see that it was an instinctive reaction.*
>
> *It is impossible to be anything other than that. I have never denied that the ball was controlled with my hand. I told the Irish players, the referee and the media this after the game. Naturally I feel embarrassed at the way that we won and feel extremely sorry for the Irish who definitely deserve to be in South Africa. Of course the fairest solution would be to replay the game but it is not in my control. There is little more I can do apart from admit that the ball had contact with my hand leading up to our equalizing goal and I feel very sorry for the Irish.*

Indeed, everything happened very quickly. However, neither Henry nor any other top player typically claims an action as unintentional when a split-second decision of theirs results in a brilliant goal, assist or save.

It is plausible the two French players did not consciously mean to be offside, nor gain some advantage from this. While technically speaking it was unlawful, morally speaking it was not. After all, the moral basis of the offside rules in football is that they exist primarily to prevent players goal-hanging.

The initial handball offence may have even been instinctive and accidental, and possibly even ball-to-hand. It is impossible to make an absolute ruling on this, but Henry can be given the benefit of the doubt here. That being said, if the referee had seen this, the only appropriate decision would have been to award a free kick to Ireland.

The second offence (or fourth, if you include the two offsides), however, is hard to excuse. Maybe it was instinctive, and maybe two days after the event, as Henry realised the implications, he could convince himself that it was not a conscious decision. But the evidence suggests that it was a deliberate act, however quickly executed, and was against the rules of the game.

Regardless of what FIFA or anyone else says, World Cup games are not like local league games in the park. There, a handball-assisted goal might be a subject for laughter and referee-baiting after the game. At the highest level, when the game's superstars are involved, there are major implications. Enormous amounts of money in sponsorships, bonuses and rewards are at stake. National team pride, and in the cases of football-mad nations such as Ireland, the hopes of a nation ride on World Cup qualification.

Henry reported discussing the statement with his lawyer before releasing it. He apparently agreed to the standard ploy of damage control. The timing of his admissions to the Irish players, his pity for the Irish, and his suggestion that the game should be replayed all came too late. The admission of the handball should have come directly after the incident, allowing Hansson to make an appropriate ruling on the play. Had this been done, the expression of sympathy and the comment about a replay would have been unnecessary – it would have never come to this stage.

Henry is not a bad person. Anyone can make a mistake. But Henry's real mistake was not the handball. His mistake was what happened afterwards. The celebrations, followed by his confession to Dunne and attempt to console the Irish player – these actions are illogical in light of each other. In an ideal world, Henry would have never handled the ball, but once the action was taken, he should have admitted his fault immediately. Unfortunately, it is only a matter of time before a similar incident happens again in an important game.

> *All that I know most surely about morality*
> *and obligations, I owe to football.*
> Albert Camus

—14—

South Africa 2010 – French revolution produces French toast

T HE SEEDING SYSTEM for the World Cup finals tournament in 2010 was yet another example of how FIFA's handling of what should have been a straightforward and visible process instead could lead to accusations of manipulation and favouritism. For previous tournaments, FIFA used a combination of factors, taking into account a country's ranking and its performances in previous finals. Rankings are computed monthly, and it had been known for a long time that the draw for the groups would take place in early December. Yet this time FIFA did not take into account performances in previous finals, nor did it use the most up-to-date rankings from November 2009. Jérôme Valcke, FIFA's general secretary, explained that "This time the feeling was the October rankings most closely represented the best teams in the tournament." So instead of consistency and transparency, the FIFA decision was based on a "feeling".

It was an extraordinary coincidence that the French were drawn in South Africa's group. Before the draw was made, the former France coach Michel Hidalgo said that it was an "injustice" that France was not among the first seeds. France and Portugal would have replaced

Argentina and England as first seeds had the November 2009 rankings been used to determine seeding rather than the October 2009 rankings. But, as luck would have it, yet again, France avoided competing against a really top team. The four teams in Group A (October 2009 ranking in parentheses) were South Africa (85), France (9), Mexico (18), and Uruguay (25). Each team in group A approached the finals with realistic hopes of making it past the group stage.

France was finally eliminated from the 2010 World Cup without having ever played a team from the top sixteen in the world. In fact, the highest-ranked team they played was Mexico (seeded 18) and the second-highest was Serbia (seeded 20), who topped their qualifying group.

It is not easy to think of a system which would satisfy all requirements, but continuing to ascribe a top seeding to the host nation regardless of its ranking creates too many imbalances and is basically unfair. These imbalances affect several teams. The host country is already favoured by not having to pre-qualify, and has in addition the significant advantage of playing at home. This should be more than enough.

Fans and commentators had six months to look forward to the World Cup finals from the time the groups were determined. It is traditional to apply a label such as the "group of death" to the group thought to be the most competitive. Based on FIFA rankings, France found themselves in a "group of life". Admittedly, such analysis can be considered speculative for many reasons. One reason is the questionable accuracy of the FIFA rankings, which is based on performance over several years and not recent performances only. Two months before France won the World Cup in 1998, it was ranked 25th on the world ranking list. Another reason is actual team form, or rather the form a team displays when it competes in the finals. There is a long interval between the end of the qualification campaign and the start of the World Cup finals. A lot can happen in these six months. Key players may suffer injuries, or loss of form, and events off the field may affect individual or team preparations, confidence and morale. On the other hand, key players may find big improvements in form, and players returning from injury can be a big boost to a team. Lastly, major football tournaments always have a number of teams which perform well above expectations, and a number which underperform. Denmark failed to qualify for the European Championship finals in Sweden in 1992, but was invited to participate after Yugoslavia was disqualified. Denmark won the event.

The French team anticipated an improvement in form for the finals. They expected a boost to be provided by the return from injury of Franck Ribéry, who was unavailable for both games against Ireland. However, most commentators identified defensive vulnerability as the key weakness that needed to be addressed. "The defence is in a permanent state of reconstruction," according to former midfielder Emmanuel Petit. It was noteworthy that Mexico (18) and Uruguay (25) were both far ahead of Ireland (ranked 34th in October 2009) in the rankings. Raymond Domenech's decision to omit Patrick Viera, Karim Benzema and Samir Nasri from the squad was somewhat controversial. Domenech planned to use Thierry Henry as a substitute, and so had to choose a new team captain. He appointed Patrice Evra. It was reported that William Gallas was unhappy that he was not selected. He was especially upset that he only found out about the decision by seeing the captain's armband beside Evra's shirt prior to the friendly against Costa Rica. Bacary Sagna supported Evra's appointment, describing him as a natural leader and one who was "desperate to set an example". That he was destined to do, but not in the way anyone would have predicted.

Traditionally, French teams have done well when their side has included a superstar at the top of his form. Just Fontaine, Michel Platini and Zinedine Zidane were such players in the past. Much would depend on how Ribéry performed, and since he did not play against the Irish, he did not have as much of the baggage of that unfair qualification to carry as others. However, he had the burden of his own personal issues to deal with, after he was among those questioned by police investigating the affairs of an underage prostitute. His lawyer later claimed that his mental balance and concentration had been "extremely destabilised" by the case.

It is difficult to assess whether the controversial manner of qualification affected the French team's performance in South Africa. Under Domenech, the French press and public have been less than enthusiastic in their support of the team. In the immediate aftermath of their undeserved qualification, the level of support fell even lower. But more than six months had passed since that night in Paris. Could the French go to the finals truly determined to win, knowing that if they did, their victory would forever be tainted by having been achieved on the back of a cheating qualification? Their games were certainly watched with great interest, and not only in France. It appeared, however, that many neutral observers shed their neutrality temporarily, to cheer for France's opponents.

If the French were hoping to distance themselves from the events of November 18th, they were repeatedly reminded of the manner of their qualification in the run-up to the finals. Even FIFA's official guide to the event made Henry's handball the focal point of the section on the French team. Prior to France's opening game against Uruguay, Domenech remained convinced that French participation in the finals was "deserved". Nevertheless, he admitted that the atmosphere in the squad was far from "calm".

France's opening game against Uruguay finished scoreless. The French were unable to take advantage of the extra man after Uruguay's Nicolas Lodeiro was sent off only 18 minutes after coming on as a substitute. The most interesting moment came late in the game when a mis-hit shot from Thierry Henry bounced off the ground on to a defender, and Henry and the French made half-hearted and unsuccessful appeals for a penalty for handball. The irony of the moment was certainly appreciated by many commentators and viewers. More importantly, the overall French performance was lacking invention, and Franck Ribéry was uninspiring.

France's next match was against Mexico, which had also drawn its opening fixture, 1–1 against South Africa. Already the margin for error for both teams was small. Neither could afford to lose and retain reasonable chances of progressing to the round of sixteen. In its first ever victory over France, Mexico won by two second-half goals to nil, and the French performance was described as "awful". Manchester United-bound striker Javier Hernandez scored Mexico's first after beating the offside trap (Hernandez's grandfather, Tomas Balcazar, had scored against France in the 1954 World Cup finals). Veteran Cuauhtemoc Blanco scored the second from the penalty spot after some woeful French defending. After the game, captain Patrice Evra said he felt that France had become "a small football nation", and, borrowing a phrase from Eamon Dunphy, acknowledged that France was "not a great team".

Raymond Domenech was seen returning to the bench after the half-time break well in advance of his players emerging, and André Pierre Gignac replaced Nicolas Anelka for the second half. What occurred in the French dressing room during the break, and its consequences, was to emerge as one of the big stories of these World Cup finals.

Two days after the Mexico game, the FFF announced that Nicolas Anelka was being sent home. It was reported in the French sports paper *L'Equipe* that he had verbally abused Domenech in the dressing room at half-time, and refused afterwards to apologise for his remarks. Worse was to follow the next day when the French team went to a scheduled training session. French captain Patrice Evra was seen arguing with fitness coach Robert Duverne. Domenech had to intervene to separate the antagonists. Duverne stormed off, flinging his credentials badge away in anger. The team returned to the bus without training.

Domenech finished meeting with the players and emerged from the bus. Bizarrely, he read a statement from the players expressing their unanimous opposition to Anelka's expulsion from the squad, omitting to mention then that he himself thought the players' action was "imbecilic". The statement's key words were "to mark the opposition to those at the highest level of French football, all the players decided not to train today". Domenech himself believed the decision to expel Anelka was "the right one", given his refusal to apologise, but criticised media coverage of the dressing-room spat for exposing "the internal life of the squad". (Irish supporters may notice interesting parallels with the Saipan incident.) Patrice Evra spoke of a "traitor" responsible for revealing details of the dressing room row between Anelka and Domenech, claiming that "There's somebody in our group that wants to harm the France team." At this point, the reader might be excused for considering that the list of possible suspects fitting this description could be very long indeed. Team director Jean-Louis Valentin announced to the attending media that the players were refusing to train, calling it a scandal. He went on, "It is a shame. As for me, it's over. I'm leaving the federation. I'm sickened and disgusted. Under these conditions, I've decided to return to Paris and to resign." The team statement criticised the FFF for making the decision about Anelka without consulting all the players, but the FFF countered by claiming that the sanction had been imposed after long discussions with the players in the presence of the players' representative, captain Patrice Evra. Christian Teinturier, vice president of the FFF, described the situation as "catastrophic" for French football. Ironically, the team's decision not to train may have been the only thing that all the players agreed upon during the entire World Cup. The team statement spoke of the "fans and countless children who keep *Les Bleus* as role models" – no doubt drawn from the 12% of the French who thought France deserved to be at the World Cup finals.

The reaction in France to these extraordinary events was scathing. *L'Equipe* wrote that Patrice Evra had "muddled up the role of captain with that of a gang leader". *Le Parisien* called the players a "band of spoilt children" and continued: "To have the worst football team at the World Cup was already unbearable. To also have the most stupid is intolerable." *Le Figaro* called it a "living nightmare". Sochaux coach Francis Gillot described the French squad's attitude as "pathetic and disgraceful", saying that France was "the laughing stock of the world".

Sports Minister Roselyne Bachelot spoke of "the indignation of the French people", and French President Nicolas Sarkozy asked her to meet with Evra, Domenech and FFF president Jean-Pierre Escalettes. Ms Bachelot referred to "the tarnished image of France" and called it a "moral disaster". She claimed her admonishments reduced some of the players to tears. Franck Ribéry bemoaned the fact that "Everyone in the whole world is mocking us now." Florent Malouda apologised to the French people, calling the refusal to train "a complete disaster". A number of team sponsors began to distance themselves from the aptly named *Les Bleus*.

Needing a resounding victory over South Africa in their final game, combined with a decisive result between Uruguay and Mexico, the French turned in another miserable performance and lost 2–1 to a team ranked more than seventy places below them. Patrice Evra was dropped for the game. Yoann Gourcuff was restored to the line-up, but probably wished he had not been, as he received a first-half red card for elbowing an opponent. Even when the final whistle blew, the controversy that dogged this campaign was not over. Raymond Domenech refused the traditional post-game handshake offered by opposing coach Carlos Alberto Parreira. He declined to clearly explain why, but it was rumoured that it was because Parreira had questioned the deservedness of France's qualification for the finals. As he departed his high-profile position as France's coach, he said, "I have had six exceptional years." No one would disagree.

The fallout continued after the team returned home. All the players forfeited their bonuses, and Thierry Henry met with President Sarkozy to provide his explanation of what happened. The President, whose reaction to the Henry handball was based on the principle that politics should not interfere in sport, was quoted as saying, "It is a political problem. When the whole world is laughing at us, it goes beyond sport." A cultural affairs committee of the National Assembly questioned Domenech, FFF president Jean-Pierre Escalettes, and others about the events in South Africa. Lawmaker Jean-François Cope said Domenech's testimony "wasn't very digni-fied". Meanwhile, FIFA was reminding the French that political interference was against FIFA's rules. Escalettes announced his resignation shortly after returning to France, citing his acceptance of his "share of the responsibility".

As further details and revelations are likely to seep out in the months and years to come, the only positive note was that a new beginning was already commencing as Laurent Blanc took over as coach. For the French, they can reasonably hope that the view expressed by *Le Figaro*'s headline after their team was finally eliminated from the World Cup ("The nightmare is finally over") is not premature.

> *Nations have their ego, just like individuals.*
> James Joyce

—15—

Whither Ireland?

REGARDLESS OF WHETHER or not football's administrators introduce effective measures to assist referees to make better decisions and to help eliminate various forms of cheating in the sport, Ireland will continue to compete at international level with optimism and pride.

For Irish football fans, thousands of whom would certainly have made the journey to South Africa had Ireland qualified, the World Cup was watched from a distance, with keen interest for a number of reasons.

Firstly, the fortunes of the French team were closely followed, and Irish supporters were not disappointed that the French exited the tournament at the earliest possible moment. While in the past there may have been a certain tendency for some supporters to hope that the team that advances at the expense of their own does well (to demonstrate how good their eliminated team really was), this hardly applied on this occasion. In some ways, France's elimination could be seen as a major step on the road to the final healing of the wounds inflicted by the events of 18th November 2009.

Secondly, England took part, and this always heightens the entertainment value of a World Cup from the Irish point of view. They get a close-up view of the British media's unique coverage of the event, as yet again England embark on the World Cup quest with the unrealistic but firmly held belief that they are in with a chance of winning outright. Such hopes are traditionally dashed by elimination at the quarter-final stage (one round earlier this time), to be followed by bitter recriminations as they try to identify the main culprit for their dashed hopes. The tabloids started early this time, and had already lined up a few potential candidates to blame by early March 2010. And of course, the Irish had three more teams to root for in the group stages.

Thirdly, the World Cup always provides enough incidents of note to remind us that competitive sport is essentially a part of the entertainment industry. Unfortunately, the South African event will likely be remembered more for its controversies than its football.

Finally, there was the football. Millions around the world saw some great goals, many highly competitive and compelling games, and plenty of drama. Sadly, the final itself was a great disappointment as a spectacle, littered with foul play and yellow cards.

After July 2010, life began anew in the world of international football. Giovanni Trapattoni has confirmed he will remain as manager, and hopes to lead Ireland to the World Cup finals in Brazil in 2014. Ireland has been handed a relatively favourable draw in the upcoming European Championship qualifiers, in a group with Russia and Slovakia as its main competitors. But the best chance of qualification is to win the group outright. UEFA has already stated in the competition regulations that the play-offs for the second-placed teams will be seeded.

Many are optimistic about the long-term prospects for the Irish team. It should certainly not be overawed by any opposition after its recent performances. Nevertheless, there are certain obvious areas where improvement is essential if the Irish are to achieve what people expect, and what they have now come to expect of themselves. It must be remembered that these heightened expectations are largely based on a single performance in a game in which they no longer had anything to lose. To be fair, we should add that the roots of this performance could be seen earlier in the 2–2 home draw with Italy, and the first-half display in Dublin against the French. Overall, Ireland's displays in the qualification group were adequate rather than impressive, and this was partly responsible for the euphoria over the performance in Paris. In addition, the exceptionally poor performances of both Italy and France do raise some important questions about the quality of the current Irish squad.

One of the traditional failings of the team has been its inability to build on a lead once established. This not only tends to induce a certain nervousness in performance, but also leaves the team wide open to dropping valuable points to late equalizers. This exact scenario was responsible for many Irish disappointments in recent years. This is an aspect of the psychological make-up of the team, a question of mental strength and toughness. There are effective ways to address this issue, but it will not go away by wishing it away. Allied to this is the suspicion of a lack of stamina, both physical and mental. Perhaps some of this is related to the fact that the team members are largely drawn from the second or third level teams in the Premier League, rather that mostly from the top four or six. (Ten of the eleven starters for France on 18th November played for clubs which had reached the round of sixteen in the 2009–2010 Champions League. Gignac of Toulouse was the exception. In contrast, only one of Ireland's starting eleven, John O'Shea, played for a Champions

League contender.) This failing may not be apparent in every game of ninety minutes, but becomes more obvious in extra time, or in tournaments. Addressing this issue in a team that gets together only intermittently for training and games is not easy, but it can be done. Ireland has played extra time three times in the World Cup (against France in November 2009, and twice at the World Cup finals, against Romania in 1990, and Spain in 2002), and never scored.

Interestingly, since the introduction of three points for a win some years ago, football strategies and tactics do not appear to have changed much. We would not expect them to alter in the small four-team groups at the final tournaments, mainly for the simple reason that all teams are essentially in contention, and a draw not only secures a point but deprives the opposition of two other possible points. However, in the larger qualifying groups, it would make eminent sense to take more risks against the teams not in contention for the top places. Such an approach could well result in two wins and a loss out of three games against such opposition (and 6 points), whereas a more cautious approach might yield two draws and a win (five points). There is less point in taking greater risks against the top teams, because it is just as important to deprive them of points as to win points.

Meanwhile, Trapattoni is well aware that while friendly games can provide the opportunity for introducing new players, the results in these games can affect a team's confidence, and are taken into consideration when computing the FIFA rankings (although friendly matches do not count for UEFA's National Team Coefficient Ranking System). Nevertheless, at this stage the Irish should be actively trying to arrange home friendly matches whenever possible. The advantages in experience gained for the players, the possibility of gradually improving our world ranking, and the opportunity for the supporters to see their heroes, outweigh any potential disadvantages. Importantly, this is best accompanied by a deliberate campaign to get the media and fans to accept these fixtures as important for our status, and to dispel the notion that such friendly games are meaningless.

In Giovanni Trapattoni, Ireland is fortunate to have a manager who is experienced, analytical and assertive. What is more, while remaining pragmatic, he is adaptable and can recognise what the situation requires. At this stage in his career, one wonders indeed what he might achieve in charge of a team with a greater depth of talent. The Irish are glad they will not find out. Above all, football is a team game, and Trapattoni remembers this when all around him tend to forget it. The really great teams of the World Cup have been, above all else, exactly that – teams: Brazil in 1970, the Netherlands in 1974, Italy in 1982. The current world champions Italy won in 2006 with ten different players scoring their twelve goals. Here too begins, and ends, our contribution to the debate about Andy Reid and Stephen Ireland.

Many of the players who played so well in Paris are young and will form the backbone of the Irish team for years to come. Kevin Doyle and Seán St Ledger can expect to represent Ireland often in the coming years, as can the midfield trio of Glenn Whelan, Keith Andrews and Liam Lawrence. Kevin Kilbane will not expect to be part of the next Irish team that plays a World Cup match. Richard Dunne, Damien Duff, Robbie Keane, John O'Shea and Shay Given may well still be there, but some of them will be past their best at that time. These have been among Ireland's top players over the past decade, and are definitely players of international quality. We can only hope that the Irish management team is able to introduce more players of the calibre of the trio of Irish players who bossed midfield in Paris. Lawrence, Whelan and Andrews all made their international debuts since Trapattoni took over as manager in May 2008. With players of the quality of Stephen Hunt not currently able to command a regular place in the team, Irish fans do have good reason to be optimistic.

The year 2009 was a tough one for the Irish: economic meltdown, rising unemployment, exposure of the extent of clerical abuse of children, severe and widespread flooding, and more besides. These are serious problems, undoubtedly much more important than what happened in Paris. In sport, there were two events in 2009 that will never be forgotten by those who witnessed them: Ireland winning the grand slam in rugby, and Ireland being eliminated from the World Cup by *that* goal. Interestingly, those watching on television were probably more traumatised by what Henry did than those at the game itself, because they had a much better view of it. Among the photographs we have included is a panoramic shot of the Irish fans in the stands at the Paris match, taken by Stephen McCarthy. One of the large flags had the words "Dallas Irish on tour" printed on the green part of the flag. On the orange section it reads "'All that matters is winning' J.R. Ewing 1978". One of the consequences of the French goal has been that football fans everywhere are perhaps less likely to believe this.

Irish football supporters are still trying to deal with their response to what happened in Paris. Several commentators pointed to the Kübler-Ross model of how people cope with loss, commonly known as the five stages of grief, as a good guide to how supporters would react. These five stages are denial, anger, bargaining, depression and acceptance. This model appears indeed to be quite applicable in the circumstances. The denial phase was immediate, and involved not only the players, but also those watching. The photograph included elsewhere in this book, showing the reaction of Irish fans to the French goal, speaks for itself. There is also no doubt that there was a phase of anger. There are reports of how the Irish players reacted in the dressing room after the game when they were shown the replays of the French goal, and the internet and newspapers were full of angry commentary in the days after the game. Typical of this anger phase is the search for someone to blame. In this instance there were many suspects: referee Martin Hansson, his assistant Fredrik Nilsson, Thierry Henry, FIFA, Sepp Blatter, Michel Platini, Shay Given, Paul McShane, and others. The bargaining phase is easy to recognise as the request for a replay, a wish to turn back the clock and relive the moments with hopefully a different outcome. The depression phase is typified by reactions like "life is unfair"; "they never wanted us to qualify anyway"; and "I will only watch rugby from now on because they use video replay technology." Finally, acceptance takes over, and the recognition that what happened cannot be changed. We move on, and we look forward to topping the group in the European qualifiers, and spending June 2014 watching Ireland compete in the World Cup finals in Brazil.

For us, writing this book has been part of the process of healing and acceptance. We hope that reading it has had the same effect.

> *Being Irish, he had an abiding sense of tragedy, which*
> *sustained him through temporary periods of joy.*
> William Butler Yeats

—16—

Bits & Pieces

Miscellaneous Quotes

Better to remain silent and be thought a fool than to speak out and remove all doubt.
    Abraham Lincoln

Oh what a tangled web we weave, when first we practise to deceive.
    Sir Walter Scott

The game is football; its first principle is that handling the ball is outlawed. That dictates everything about how the sport is played. Handle the ball – in doing so claiming one of the greatest prizes – and you strike a blow at the very heart of football.
    Jim Holden (*World Soccer*)

It was necessary to exploit what was exploitable.
    Thierry Henry

Well done, Thierry. Not only do you bend the rules to breaking point, you then blame somebody else for letting you get away with it!
    Mark Ogden (*The Telegraph*)

In the specific case of the Henry handball, the referee (Martin Hansson) should have taken the time to reflect rather than immediately awarding the goal.
    Sepp Blatter

Handball!

Except for this terrible mistake, it was I think one of the best games I have refereed in my career.
Martin Hansson on the France–Ireland game.

We've put a man on the moon and we can't see if the ball has hit a hand.
Harry Redknapp

Football is full of heroes who have cheated ten times more than Thierry.
Arsène Wenger

The highest crime in football is touching the ball with the hands.
Sepp Blatter, on 30th November 2009.

You know, I've known William a long time. I don't want to make this nostalgia night but we went to school together, we share the same date of birth; we were at Clairefontaine together. To come together with him in that move, both of us, was a big moment. It will go down in history.
Thierry Henry on William Gallas, and their goal.

So if you're a sporting hero and would like to remain that way ... don't single-handedly piss off an entire country.
Patrick Horan (tribune.ie)

He said he scored with his shoulder.
Arsène Wenger telling us what William Gallas said to him about the goal that put Ireland out of the World Cup.

With the first handball, I didn't even know it hit me. It was after I saw it that I had the bad reflex. Liza, I swear to you, the first time I didn't even know it hit my hand.
Thierry Henry, explaining to Bixente Lizarazu.

What the hell is Richard Dunne sitting next to that p**** for?
Irish supporter at the Stade de France (reported by Richard Sadlier, *Sunday Independent*).

If he could have it all over again, he wouldn't do it.
  Kevin Moran, on Thierry Henry (*RTE*)

Loss of money – nothing lost. Loss of health – much lost. Loss of honour – all lost.
  Chinese proverb

I've lost all respect for him as a sportsperson.
  Eoin Hand, former Irish manager, on Thierry Henry (*RTE*)

I shouldn't have done that but, frankly, it was uncontrollable, after all we had been through.
  Thierry Henry, on celebrating the goal (*L'Equipe*)

When I was a centre forward in my junior team, I definitely gained an advantage by pulling a defender's jersey in order to score a goal. And I didn't go and see the referee to tell him about it.
  Sepp Blatter

So he goes to South Africa, but he goes there with a heavy heart, torn and unhappy and tormented. He goes there questioning the meaning of life. As anyone who has ever seen one of their awful movies will attest, this is how the French like to do it.
  Brendan O'Connor (*Sunday Independent*)

It made me furious that Thierry can be treated this way, I have not slept for two days and I am just starting to get over it.
  Raymond Domenech

Most people don't like him, so being a fan of Domenech is more original than liking Nelson Mandela, the Beatles or chocolate ice cream.
  Patrick Vignal (*Reuters Soccer Blog*)

Handball!

Henry is probably beginning to realise that he picked the wrong crowd to try to swindle. The Irish know how to hold a grudge and this won't be forgotten. Ask the English.

Keith Duggan (*The Irish Times*)

In sport as in life, you don't always get what you deserve. Sport has more in common with Hamlet *than with* Eastenders.

Eamonn Sweeney (*Sunday Independent*)

If the FFF was running Irish football, Steve Staunton would still be manager.

Dion Fanning (*Sunday Independent*)

But no, not content with stealing the last éclair, he had to try to eat it right there in front of us. The commiserating with Richard Dunne, the preposterous call for a replay after FIFA had confirmed the result would stand, the whinging that he had considered quitting the game ("I felt alone"... enough, mon dieu).

Patrick Horan, on Thierry Henry (tribune.ie)

I can tell you, from the experience with my handball, I was all alone and I know what it feels like.

Thierry Henry (interviewed on French TV about Nicolas Anelka's treatment in South Africa)

I don't see what we could have done better. We needed to qualify and we did that, even if it was painful. Victories like this one, at the end of a difficult campaign, give this side heart and soul.

Raymond Domenech

Maradona could not kick with his right foot and did not score with his head. The only time he scored an important goal with his head, he used his hand.

Pelé, discussing the offence of handball

In the case of Thierry Henry's handling of the ball . . . an entire nation has taken on the role of unjustly oppressed victim – something the Irish do well, having had several centuries of practice.

Dominic Lawson (*Sunday Times*)

I want to pay tribute to the Irish team and their fans, what they did over two matches – they gave us a lot of problems and I want to congratulate them. I'm disappointed for them and their public. But bravo to them.

Raymond Domenech

Keane, you will recall, believes everybody in Ireland should shut up whining and blame Shay Given for the defeat to France, partly because the Irish goalkeeper didn't come and collect the cross from which William Gallas scored and mainly because Roy Keane doesn't like him.

Harry Pearson (guardian.co.uk)

Some of his calls were strange. Maybe next time I'll learn how to dive. I expect the referee to do his job but I don't think he did. In fact, I'd like to have seen a proper referee out there.

Thierry Henry, after Arsenal was defeated by Barcelona in the 2006 Champions League final.

At this stage not taking video evidence is tantamount to the referee running away from protesting players, with his fingers in his ears, shouting: "La la la, I'm not listening, I'm not listening."

Dara O'Briain (guardian.co.uk)

I was bitterly disappointed and upset about what happened in Paris [but] the saddest thing is we would have all taken it if it had happened for us. We'd have watched the World Cup if it was Ireland and forgotten about it. It's a sad indictment on all of us that we accept it.

Mick McCarthy

Patriotism is the last refuge of a scoundrel.

Samuel Johnson (1709–1784)

Handball!

"I will always give 101 per cent in every situation," he [Trapattoni] said, leaving some of us wondering what happened the missing nine. Worrying.
   Mary Hannigan (*The Irish Times*)

It was hard, laborious and indeed miraculous. I was sure we would make it though. My forecast was 1–1!
   Raymond Domenech

To the chagrin of those members of the French football populace with a con-science, Raymond Domenech did exactly what they would have expected of him in the aftermath of France's unheroic journey to the World Cup finals. He made everyone cringe.
   Amy Lawrence (guardian.co.uk)

... a random Frenchman, let's call him ... Michel Platini, say, may not have noticed that such a controversy has arisen, and has therefore not felt the need to comment on it. This would surprise many people given that such a Frenchman was previously known to get on his high horse ("un cheval de haute") about all sorts of injustices in sport.
   Dara O'Briain (guardian.co.uk)

Had an Irish team of football supporting lawyers been let loose on the case, they might well have sought to prosecute it on the basis of Article 54 which deals with "Provoking the general public"; Article 57: "Offensive behaviour and fair play" or, indeed, Section 5: "Forgery and falsification."
   Emmet Malone, after FIFA said they had no legal basis to sanction Henry (*The Irish Times*).

I have not finished my mission in soccer, I need more time. I hope that in 2011 the FIFA Congress has further faith in me, otherwise I'll go back to my village.
   Sepp Blatter

The truth is rarely pure and never simple.
   Oscar Wilde

Instead, he [Sepp Blatter] tried to tackle the sensitive issue of Henry's malfea-sance by introducing more match officials, thus adding to the enjoyment of fans by increasing the number of refs they can abuse by close to 50%.

Harry Pearson (guardian.co.uk)

Integrity has no need of rules.

Albert Camus

It has been a strange fortnight. The French, in fairness, behaved impecca-bly in all of this, diving into a bout of national introspection and talking about the whole thing like the Dreyfus affair had come to life again. It was kind of enjoyable, to be honest, listening to a succession of suave French folks talking on Irish radio about their shame and about the nobility of the Irish team. It almost made the trauma of losing worth it.

Keith Duggan (*The Irish Times*)

Chronic remorse, as all moralists are agreed, is a most undesirable sentiment. If you have behaved badly, repent, make what amends you can and address yourself to the task of behaving better next time. On no account brood over your wrongdoing. Rolling in the muck is not the best way of getting clean.

Aldous Huxley (in a 1946 foreword to *Brave New World*)

I knew it was tight – probably about two metres!

German goalkeeper Manuel Manuel Neuer on Frank Lampard's "goal" against Germany in South Africa

Every four years people say England will win the World Cup. What happens? They don't win it and they get hammered for six months – and then they say okay, we will win the next one.

Arsène Wenger

Soccer is more than just a business. No one has their ashes scattered down the aisle at Tesco.

Professor Rogan Taylor, a Liverpool fan

Handball!

It's so lonely 'round the fields of a T. Henry.
    Comment on guardian.co.uk

Poor Thierry has got his reward for Paris. Namely a bit-part in a horror movie. If that's not karma, what is?
    Vincent Hogan (*Irish Independent*)

After refusing to play against Uruguay and Mexico, the French players have now refused to practise.
    Vincent Duluc (*L'Equipe*)

Zinedine Kilbane.
    Irish supporters on Kevin Kilbane's silky skills

We'll always have Paris.
Humphrey Bogart in *Casablanca*

Sweet Memories

When someone says, "It has taken me a long time to forget this or that", it inevitably means they have not forgotten it, as in the Bob Dylan song, "Most of the Time". Henry's handball brought back many memories.

- Trapattoni and the Italian press recalled a referee called Byron Moreno from 2002.
- The Spaniards recalled their defeat to South Korea from the same year.
- Roy Keane recalled an exotic location called Saipan from the same year.
- Pelé recalled his ongoing point-scoring competition with Maradona for the greatest-footballer-ever title.
- The English recalled Maradona's "hand of God" goal in 1986.
- The Germans recalled England's third goal in the World Cup final of 1966.
- The FFF recalled every unfair decision that had ever gone against the French team.

The memory plays tricks too. There appear to be certain myths already taking root as to what happened in Paris on 18th November 2009. The first is that Ireland was winning the tie at the time Gallas scored, and already on the way to qualification. They were winning the game, but the tie was level at 1–1. The second is that the goal will be remembered as Henry's goal, and not Gallas'. Already in February 2010, Olympic Council of Ireland president Patrick Hickey was quoted as saying, "We're already suffering from the football . . . Thierry Henry scoring a goal with his hand and eliminating us from the World Cup finals."

> *"History is the lies we agree on."*
> Voltaire

The ten most infuriating aspects of Ireland's elimination from the 2010 World Cup (in no particular order) were ...

- FIFA's failure to mention the handball in its match report.
- Martin Hansson claiming 100% certainty there was no handball.
- Thierry Henry celebrating Gallas' goal.
- Raymond Domenech complaining his enjoyment of qualification was spoiled by controversy.
- Ireland's failure to take one of its many chances to score a decisive second goal in normal time.
- Thierry Henry consoling Richard Dunne on the pitch.
- FIFA seeding the play-off draw.
- Roy Keane blaming the Irish defense for Gallas' goal.
- Thierry Henry supporting calls for a replay after it had been ruled out.
- Reading the FIFA Fair Play code after the game.

Handball!

World Cup Trivia

- The first goal ever scored at the World Cup finals was by a Frenchman, Lucien Laurant. He scored the opening goal when France defeated Mexico 4–1 in Uruguay on 13th July 1930.
- The first player ever to score four goals in any World Cup match was Paddy Moore of Ireland, against Belgium in a qualifier in Dublin 1934. The game finished 4–4.
- Uruguay was the only holder of the World Cup that did not defend its title. They won the first World Cup in 1930, but did not play in the 1934 event.
- Italy had to qualify to participate in the 1938 World Cup, which they hosted.
- Brazil omitted top scorer Leônidas da Silva from their semi-final line-up against Italy in 1938, after manager Ademar Pimenta decided to rest him for the final. Italy won 2–1, and went on to win the final.
- There was no World Cup final in 1950. Brazil and Uruguay met in the last match of a group phase to decide the winner. Brazil needed a draw to become champions. Uruguay won the game 2–1.
- There was an unusual seeding system in the group phase in 1954. The top two seeds in each group only played two games, against the unseeded teams.
- Only three teams, England, Uruguay and Spain, have never lost a World Cup final in which they participated.
- Two teams have played twice in a World Cup final without ever winning the World Cup; Czechoslovakia in 1934 and 1962, and Hungary in 1938 and 1954. The Netherlands is the only team to have played three times in the final without winning (1974, 1978 and 2010).
- The record for the most consecutive appearances in a World Cup final is shared between (West) Germany (1982, 1986 and 1990) and Brazil (1994, 1998 and 2002).

- In the 1970 World Cup finals, Mexico scored after taking a free-kick awarded to El Salvador!

- The original World Cup, the Jules Rimet trophy, was won outright by Brazil in 1970. It had been stolen prior to the World Cup in England in 1966, but was recovered by a dog named Pickles. It was stolen again in Brazil in 1983, and was never recovered.

- Ireland reached the World Cup quarter-finals in Italy in 1990 without winning a game (they overcame Romania only on penalties in the round of 16, following three draws in the group phase).

- In 1994, three points for a win was introduced. This was supposed to encourage more attacking football. The average number of goals per game increased from 2.21 (1990) to 2.71 (1994), but has been gradually declining since then.

Table 5. Average number of goals per game at the World Cup finals.

Year	Goals/game	Year	Goals/game
1930	3.88	1978	2.68
1934	4.12	1982	2.81
1938	4.67	1986	2.54
1950	4.00	1990	2.21
1954	5.38	1994	2.71
1958	3.60	1998	2.67
1962	2.78	2002	2.52
1966	2.78	2006	2.30
1970	2.97	2010	2.27
1974	2.55		

- Three countries failed to score a single goal at the World Cup finals in 2002: defending champions France, China and Saudi Arabia.
- When Brazil played Germany in the World Cup final in Japan in 2002, it was the first time ever that the teams had met in the World Cup (although Brazil had played against East Germany in 1974).
- Three teams hold the record for the most players red-carded during a World Cup finals tournament. Argentina (1990), Cameroon (1998) and France (1998), all had three players sent off.
- Yellow cards were introduced in time for the World Cup finals in 1970.

Table 6. Red and yellow cards
at the World Cup finals since 1970.

Year	Games played	Red cards	Yellow cards
1970	32	0	52
1974	38	5	86
1978	38	3	58
1982	52	5	98
1986	52	8	137
1990	52	16	169
1994	52	15	235
1998	64	22	258
2002	64	17	272
2006	64	28	345
2010	64	17	261

- The top three teams in the World Cup have been Brazil, (West) Germany and Italy. There have been only three World Cup finals which did not include one of the top three: the first one in 1930 between Uruguay and Argentina, the 1978 final between Argentina and the Netherlands, and the 2010 final between Spain and the Netherlands.

- The ten countries which have amassed the most points in the World Cup finals are: Brazil, (West) Germany, Italy, Argentina, England, Spain, France, the Netherlands, Uruguay and Sweden. When one of the top ten teams has hosted the World Cup finals (1930, 1934, 1938, 1950, 1958, 1966, 1974, 1978, 1982, 1990, 1998, 2006), it has won the competition on six occasions (out of twelve), and finished runners-up three times, and third twice. These figures suggest that if one of the top ten teams hosts the World Cup, it has a 50% likelihood of winning the event.

We hope you have enjoyed this book, and welcome any comments you might have. Please email us at: 18november09@gmail.com